D1190387

SEEING
AND
WRITING

BOOKS OF VERSE

ALSO BY

WALKER GIBSON

The Reckless Spenders (1954)
Come As You Are (1958)

Chartres Cathedral

SEEING
AND
WRITING

Fifteen Exercises
in
Composing Experience

❧

WALKER GIBSON
by
NEW YORK UNIVERSITY

1959

Longmans, Green and Co.

NEW YORK · LONDON · TORONTO

LONGMANS, GREEN AND CO., INC.
119 WEST 40TH STREET, NEW YORK 18

LONGMANS, GREEN AND CO., LTD.
6 & 7 CLIFFORD STREET, LONDON W 1

LONGMANS, GREEN AND CO.
20 CRANFIELD ROAD, TORONTO 16

SEEING AND WRITING

COPYRIGHT © 1959

BY LONGMANS, GREEN AND CO., INC.

PUBLISHED SIMULTANEOUSLY IN THE DOMINION OF CANADA BY
LONGMANS, GREEN AND CO., TORONTO

FIRST EDITION

LIBRARY OF CONGRESS CATALOG CARD NUMBER 59–7142

Printed in the United States of America

TO

J. B.

"I think the students should
entertain *me!*"

PREFACE

This is a book of fifteen exercises in writing for college students. Its assumption is that if young writers are encouraged to look hard at their own experience they will see something there and say something about it of interest to their teachers. It may be that teachers of college composition who are bored by their students' writing deserve what they get. This book proposes that students can be so directed to express themselves that they will inform, entertain, and instruct their instructors.

A liberally educated man is a talker and a writer, a composer of words. He is a man who can change his voice without losing track of himself: for him the terms of the historian and the scientist and the poet are all available ways of ordering a world, and their variety does not frighten him. In this book a systematic attempt is made to place the student in positions where he must see his experience from shifting points of view, and must change his terms and his tone of voice as he does so. That such an effort may lead to the student's "finding himself" is a promise that probably no teacher should make, though it is worth repeating here that most of us find ourselves only after we have spent some time getting lost first.

The liberally educated man, moreover, knows his limits. He knows, for example, that the words he uses are not identical with the things he sees, and he writes accordingly with modesty, good humor, and careful courage—in other words, with *style*. "It is style," Robert Oppenheimer has written, "which complements affirmation with limitation and with humility; it is style which makes it possible to act effectively, but not absolutely; it is style which enables us to find a harmony between the pursuit of ends essential to us, and a regard for the views, the sensibilities, the aspirations of those to whom the problem may appear in another light; it is style which is the deference that action pays to uncertainty; it is above all style through which power defers to reason." One purpose of this book is to encourage in the student some uses of style, however humble, in that sense.

The organization of the book is very simple. The first three themes explore various acts of "seeing" one's experience; the remaining exercises are grouped in a series of pairs that require re-examinations of experience in new terms. Thus Theme 4 asks for an account of a family conflict in the student's own life, while Theme 5 demands a rewriting, or "reseeing," of this conflict in the terms of an anthropologist. Theme 6 invites an anecdote of the student's school days; Theme 7 asks him to resee his relations with his teachers by using some language of a psychologist. Theme 8 asks for a simple description of a building—the façade of a neighborhood church; Theme 9 requires a new look at this façade with a historian's vocabulary; while in Theme 10 the student must examine critically his own historical assumptions. For Theme 11 the student writes an impressionistic report of the wind; for Theme 12 he sees his wind new, in statistical terms, by experimenting with a homemade anemometer that he constructs himself; and in Theme 13 he faces the limitations of his own "human standpoint" as a measurer of nature. Theme 14 offers a related practical exercise in critical reading, taken from a daily newspaper. In the final exercise certain aspects of the writer's problem are summarized by way of philosophical implications in modern physics, and the student is asked to resee in this light his own activity as a composer of themes.

Passages for reading have been kept very brief. In most cases they precede the directions for writing, their purpose being to introduce various terms and points of view for the information and encouragement of the student. But in no sense is Imitation of

Great Writers intended. There is no thought that after reading
Mark Twain on the Mississippi, the student should write like
Mark Twain—except that he should see his own Mississippi in
his own backyard.

Some observations of a practical sort are due the prospective
teacher. The intention is that each of these exercises might represent part of one week's work in a composition course, together
with whatever lessons in rhetoric, supplementary reading, use
of the library, and so on the teacher may wish to assign. But the
weekly theme is by no means the only appropriate schedule, and
the work might properly go either faster or slower. The series
can probably be completed comfortably in one semester, with
themes of perhaps five hundred words each, but it is quite conceivable that a teacher might wish to handle the material more
deliberately, with additional reading, perhaps requiring themes
of greater length. By and large it would seem best to offer the
exercises in an order close to the one given, though this too need
not be inflexible. If a shorter series is desired, certain themes can
be omitted, but they should be chosen carefully; for example,
both 4 and 5 could be omitted, but not one without the other.
In the latter part of the book, a streamlined course with good
students might dispense with 10, 13, or 14 (or even all three)
without doing great violence to the sequence of ideas. *It is particularly important that no new theme should be assigned until
the previous one has been discussed and returned to the student.*
The choice of reading passages is, of course, one man's choice;
the list can certainly be improved by each teacher's ingenuity as
his needs suggest. Each selection moreover can be approached
in a number of ways that differ from the one suggested in
the text, and the essentially empirical character of these assignments generally should not discourage the teacher from consider-
ing the literary or aesthetic aspects of the material if he so desires.
The teacher's own resourcefulness in response to his local situa-

tion is especially necessary in the assignments on the language of history (Themes 9–10) and the language of science (Themes 12–13). Here there is an opportunity to make some contact between the student's English class and his other courses, and, if these exercises can involve relevant selections from the student's own textbooks in history and science, so much the better. It is always a pleasant surprise when the words of one course can make sense in another.

In any case it seems to the compiler improbable that any one teacher would wish to pursue the precise pattern laid out in this book for longer than two or three years consecutively, assuming he could abide it that long. After such a period, it's to be hoped, he would want to apply some of the techniques exemplified here to his own materials, with his own emphasis.

It will be noticed that the book repeatedly emphasizes the difficulties of the writer's art rather than its satisfactions—the gap between word and thing rather than their successful association with one another. Such an emphasis may seem overly self-conscious, or even discouraging, to the student. But it is deliberate. To any teacher of English it is obvious that words both do and don't adequately represent experience, but only the first of these alternatives is obvious to the student. No one is so satisfied with the state of his language as the innocent who knows nothing about it. Therefore, if this book seems to "accentuate the negative," it is because that seems to be what young writers need. In an alarming passage at the end of this book, P. W. Bridgman describes a situation in which "the only way of reacting is to shut up." But no one shuts up really—certainly not Professor Bridgman himself. The danger run by all writers, including the present one, is not an excess of humility but quite the opposite.

During the past couple of years most of these assignments have been performed, more or less successfully, by freshmen at Wash-

ington Square College of New York University. I am grateful
to all these freshmen, and to the staff of English H1 at Washington Square, for putting up so cheerfully with the exercises in
their experimental stages. I am also fundamentally indebted to
my ten years of teaching in the English Department at Amherst
College, and particularly to Professors Theodore Baird and G.
Armour Craig, who taught me much of what I think I know
about the teaching of composition.

                                                                    W. G.

Contents

No method nor discipline can supersede the necessity of being forever on the alert. What is a course of history, or philosophy, or poetry, or the most admirable routine of life, compared with the discipline of looking always at what is to be seen? Will you be a reader, a student merely, or a seer? Read your fate, see what is before you, and walk on into futurity.

—THOREAU

1

SEEING THINGS

The most obvious aspect of the field of actual experience is its disorderly character. To grasp this fundamental truth is the first step in wisdom.

—WHITEHEAD

What do you want to accomplish as a writer, as a student of writing in a composition course? You might try to list some of your aims. For example, you might say that you want to convey your thoughts to others through a skillful use of words. You want to communicate clearly so that other people will really grasp your meaning. You want to express yourself, accurately, vividly. These are reasonable aims, you might say, for a course in composition.

But as a matter of fact they are not reasonable at all—they are impossible. Consider your own thoughts, for instance, and your desire to convey them to others. What *are* your thoughts? Think about your own thinking for a moment—think about your own thinking right *now*. What is in your mind? You are sitting in a chair, probably, just slightly aware of its touch on you, just slightly aware that it is or isn't upholstered. You are aware of being alone (or not alone), of the time, the temperature, the state of your stomach. How many thoughts are competing in your head, now that you think of them? A date, a game, the shape of this sentence, sleepiness, anxiety, boredom. Life! The more you think about your thinking, the more it's a mess. And if you ask yourself, now, what has happened to the state of your mind since you started thinking about it like this, your answer would have to be that it has certainly changed by the very process of trying to express it. Were you really aware of your hunger a minute ago, or is it just that you are now, being reminded of it? The more we try to describe our thoughts at a given moment, the more we do them an injustice by that very effort.

The state of our minds, as it really is at this moment, is inexpressible, and we can't "convey" that state to anybody, not even to ourselves.

Well, then, what *is* expressible? It would be possible to say, in answer to that question, that strictly speaking nothing is, that no idea can be "conveyed" precisely from the mind of one person to the mind of another. Yet we need only look around us to admire the proofs of some kind of communicating going on in the world. The business of the day gets done, on the whole marvelously well. Airplanes take off, often on time, and they land safely in dense fog without ever seeing the ground. Someone has been talking to someone else, and, if he has not expressed the state of his thoughts, he has at least gotten something done. A man in the dark, watching the pips on a radar screen, tells the pilot that he should lower his wheels, that he is nearing the runway, that he is all right—and this miracle of communication is enough to silence any skepticism.

But the practical question that confronts us in the situation of the composition class is still unanswered. What shall we write about? If we can't convey "ourselves" and the state of our minds, and if we aren't landing planes in a fog, what alternatives do we have in our search for useful problems of communication? What area of experience can we examine as a fruitful and controllable field for expression?

There are probably many answers to this question: the one adopted by this book is an obvious one. It proposes that we begin by *looking* at something simple, or at any rate something that seems simple, and that we try to render an experience of this thing in words. What do we do in the face of a scene that stands before our eyes? What do we look at? What words do we choose to express to somebody else our experience of *seeing* something? That is the problem of your first theme.

DIRECTIONS FOR THEME I

CHOOSE A PARTICULAR SCENE OR OBJECT ON YOUR CAMPUS, OR TAKE ONE ASSIGNED BY YOUR INSTRUCTOR (YOUR ROOM, A BUILDING, A STREET CORNER, PERHAPS SIMPLY A BLACKBOARD OR A PENCIL). EXPRESS AS THOROUGHLY AS YOU CAN WITHIN YOUR SPACE LIMITS WHAT YOU SEE WHEN YOU LOOK AT THIS THING.

Now here are two short passages of writing in which two English authors *see* a city street, each in his particular way. The first is a wartime impression by the novelist, Elizabeth Bowen. The second is a poem written in the thirties by Louis MacNeice.

London, 1940

by ELIZABETH BOWEN

Early September morning in Oxford Street. The smell of charred dust hangs on what should be crystal pure air. Sun, just up, floods the once more innocent sky, strikes silver balloons and the intact building-tops. The whole length of Oxford Street, west to east, is empty, looks polished like a ballroom, glitters with smashed glass. Down the distances, natural mists of morning are brown with the last of smoke. Fumes still come from the shell of a shop. At this corner where the burst gas main flaming floors high made a scene like a hell in the night, you still feel heat. The silence is now the enormous thing—it appears to amaze the street. Sections and blocks have been roped off; there is no traffic; the men in the helmets say not a person may pass (but some sneak through). Besides the high explosives that did the work, this quarter has been seeded with timebombs—so we are herded, waiting for these to go off. This is the top of Oxford Street, near where it joins the corner of Hyde Park at Marble Arch.

We people have come up out of the ground, or out from the bottom floors of the damaged houses: we now see what we heard happen throughout the night. Roped away from the rest of London we seem to be on an island—when shall we be taken off? Standing, as might the risen dead in the doors of tombs, in the mouths of the shelters, we have nothing to do but yawn at each other or down the void of streets, meanwhile rubbing the smoke-smart deeper into our eyes with our dirty fists. . . . It has been a dirty night. The side has been ripped off one near block—the open gash is nothing but dusty, colourless. (As bodies shed blood buildings shed mousy dust.) Up there the sun strikes a mirror over a mantelpiece; shreds of a carpet sag out over the void. An A. R. P. man, like a chamois, already runs up the debris; we stare. The charred taint thickens everyone's lips and tongues—what we want is bacon and eggs, coffee. We attempt little sorties—'Keep BACK, please! Keep OFF the street!' The hungry try to slake down with smoking. 'PLEASE— that cigarette *out!* Main gone—gas all over the place—d'*you* want to blow up London.' Cigarette trodden guiltily into the trodden glass. We loaf on and on in our cave-mouths; the sun goes on and on up. Some of us are dressed, some of us are not: pyjama-legs show below overcoats. There are some Poles, who having lost everything all over again sit down whenever and wherever they can. They are our seniors in this experience: we cannot but watch them. There are two or three unmistakable pairs of disturbed lovers—making one think 'Oh yes, how odd—love.' There are squads of ageless 'residents' from aquarium-like private hotels just around the corner. There are the nomads of two or three nights ago who, having been bombed out of where they were, pitched on this part, to be bombed out again. There is the very old gentleman wrapped up in the blanket, who had been heard to say, humbly, between the blasts in the night, 'The truth is, I have outlived my generation. . . .' We are none of us—except perhaps the Poles?—the very very poor: our predicament is not a great predicament. The lady in the fur coat has hair in two stiff little bedroomy grey plaits. She appeals for hair-pins: most of us have short hair—pins for her are extracted from one of the Poles' heads. Girls stepping further into the light look into pocket mirrors. 'Gosh,' they say remotely. Two or three people have, somehow, begun walking when one time-bomb goes off at Marble Arch. The street puffs itself empty; more glass splinters. Everyone laughs.

It is a fine morning and we are still alive.

This is the buoyant view of it—the theatrical sense of safety, the steady breath drawn. We shall be due, at to-night's siren, to feel our hearts once more tighten and sink. Soon after black-out we keep that date with fear. The howling ramping over the darkness, the lurch of the barrage opening, the obscure throb in the air. We *can* go underground—but for this to be any good you have to go very deep, and a number of us, fearful of being buried, prefer not to. Our own 'things'—tables, chairs, lamps—give one kind of confidence to us who stay in our own paper rooms. But when to-night the throb gathers over the roof we must not remember what we looked at this morning—these fuming utter glissades of ruin. No, these nights in September nowhere is pleasant. Where you stay is your own choice, how you feel is your fight.

However many people have crowded together, each has, while air whistles and solids rock, his or her accesses of solitude. We can do much for each other, but not all. Between bomb and bomb we are all together again: we all guess, more or less, what has been happening to all the others. Chatter bubbles up; or there is a cosy slumping sideways, to doze. Fear is not cumulative: each night it starts from scratch. On the other hand, resistance becomes a habit. And, better, it builds up a general fund.

Morning Sun

by LOUIS MacNEICE

Shuttles of trains going north, going south, drawing
    threads of blue,
The shining of the lines of trams like swords,
Thousands of posters asserting a monopoly of the good, the
    beautiful, the true.
Crowds of people all in the vocative, you and you,
The haze of the morning shot with words.

Yellow sun comes white off the wet streets but bright
Chromium yellows in the gay sun's light,
Filleted sun streaks the purple mist,
Everything is kissed and reticulated with sun
Scooped-up and cupped in the open fronts of shops
And bouncing on the traffic which never stops.

And the street fountain blown across the square
Rainbow-trellises the air and sunlight blazons
The red butcher's and scrolls of fish on marble slabs,
Whistle bars of music crossing silver sprays
And horns of cars, touché, touché, rapiers' retort, a mov-
    ing cage,
A turning page of shine and sound, the day's maze.

And when the sun goes out, the streets go cold, the hang-
    ing meat
And tiers of fish are colourless and merely dead,
And the hoots of cars neurotically repeat and the tiptoed
    feet

Of women hurry and falter whose faces are dead;
And I see in the air but not belonging there
The blown grey powder of the fountain grey as the ash
That forming on a cigarette covers the red.

It has been remarked, with truth, that before you can see
something you have to have a point of view. It will be useful
for you to try to fix the "point" from which these two London
street scenes are "viewed." Can you sense, first, a physical location, a *point,* where the person speaking seems to have stood?
In Miss Bowen's description we are told exactly where this point
is, both in time and in space. It is in the mouth of a shelter, at
the top of Oxford Street, in London, on an early morning in
September, 1940. All this information comes to us almost inci-
dentally, and is not complete until the third sentence of the second paragraph, but eventually it does come to us. (Why was
the point not defined in the very first sentence, do you suppose?)
All the objects described by the speaker are those that might
reasonably be seen from this chosen point, the mouth of a shelter,
at this particular time. Certain things are not included because
they can't be seen from this point—what is happening in the
next street, for instance.

But the phrase, "point of view," is also used metaphorically,
of course, to mean "attitude" or "frame of reference" or "value
judgment" or "interpretation." For example, in MacNeice's
poem the very way the words were selected for their sound has
an influence on point of view in this sense, on the whole attitude
toward the scene that the speaker is adopting. The morning is
"shot with words" and so is the poet! The sun he sees as
"scooped-up and cupped"; "touché, touché", he cries, "the day's
maze." His point of view here is finally not terribly solemn, because he is having such a fine time making his almost nursery-
rhyme rhythms and sound effects. Even the sad end is not really
very tragic, partly because the metaphor he has chosen to de-

scribe the "grey" fountain is only, after all, a homely old cigarette.

In Miss Bowen's piece of writing, though, the speaker is en-
gaged in no such high jinks: this is wartime, this is prose, things
are serious, and so is the point of view. Notice how the very first
sentence, which is not a sentence according to grammar books,
suggests a kind of note-taking, as if to imply, "I'm just telling you
what I see, just as I see it, with no clowning around." And how
does the speaker see it? Actually with great care and craft, and
a successful effort to avoid bathos in a situation that is danger-
ously loaded with pity and sentiment. "Girls stepping further into
the light look into pocket mirrors. 'Gosh,' they say remotely."
This sounds like the plainest and most pedestrian way to put it
down perhaps, but why do they say it "remotely"? Does that
suggest anything about the girls' state of mind, about the speaker's
relation to them, about the whole situation?

You might ask yourself whether, in your own Theme 1, you
adopted and held a more or less consistent point of view, in both
senses. Did you, first, take up a particular position, in space and
time, with reference to your scene so that your reader could see
(so far as possible) with your eyes from your vantage point?
(Did you wander, did you unnecessarily skip around?) And did
you, second, "take a stand" in the metaphorical sense: did you
assume a particular attitude toward your scene so that your
reader can "see" with you its meaning, its significance for you?

In order to see something "thoroughly," as Theme 1 so ambi-
tiously demands, you don't see everything, for no one can do
that. To convey the whole scene with all its parts into someone
else's mind is as impossible as it is to convey your thoughts into
someone else's mind. In fact they are the same thing! A point
of view is a way of limiting, a way of deciding what to select
out of the mass of impressions that any scene presents to your
eye. In order to decide what your point of view is, you have to
decide what it is you are trying to do, what it is you want your

reader to do. This means that you must go beyond the language of the assignment and refine the adverb "thoroughly" by translating it into some other adverb more practically useful for your purposes. Do you want to view your scene solemnly or gaily, sweetly or tough-mindedly? And so on. Whatever you do, you must take your stand, in both meanings of that phrase, and see your world deliberately from a particular angle of vision.

Theme 1 could be revised and rewritten, in the light of these matters, as many times as you think you and your instructor can endure it.

2

SEEING WITHOUT EYES

"I see," said the blind man, but he really didn't see at all.

We have observed that to "see" something involves a lot more than a visual act and a simple translation of this act into words. The process is complicated. You have to decide on such things as a point of view, a purpose, an audience. You have to make a number of choices, both in the scene before your eyes and in the words you employ to your reader. In a very real sense, when you look at something and talk about it, you are making it. You create the world before you by the choices you commit yourself to. From hour to hour during any day of your life, you live in a world of frivolity or solemnity, variety or monotony, depending on how you choose to "look" at it. It is this aspect of looking as interpretation that is important to the writer, rather than of looking as a mere response of the visual nerves. In fact, the use of the words seeing, observing, examining, and so on to refer to mental acts of interpreting is very common in our language: for example, *look* at the first verb in this paragraph.

It is the choice, then, of the means of interpretation that creates the world we "see"—not simply the retinas of our eyes.

For that matter, a world of great complexity and detail can be enjoyed, can be seen, without any eyes at all. That is the point of the two passages that follow. The first is by two experts on blindness (one of whom is blind), and it tells something of the curious way in which the world most of us think we live in is defined by the limited point of view of eyesight.

Sight and Light

by HECTOR CHEVIGNY and SYDELL BRAVERMAN

From the entrance of an apartment building fronting on a small city square, a man emerges holding a dog on a leash. It is a male, a small bull terrier with a broad, flat nose and a quizzical expression. Whether the dog's expression is quizzical to another dog is problematic; the dog's face conveys that impression with certainty only to the man. Man and dog are relieved to be outdoors. It is a lovely day, chilly but sunny. The skies are blue and clear. The old buildings that front the square look a little less dingy than usual; the deposit of city grime and soot on them looks almost beautiful. Upon the nature of the difference between beauty and ugliness, however, neither man nor dog pauses to think.

They cross to the little park in the center of the square. A small patch of grass lies there; a few flowers in beds are growing bravely; the trees are budding. The dog pulls his master along from object to upright object, smelling each of them carefully. He inspects the lampposts, the trees, the fire hydrants. It is quite evident that he enjoys doing this. After a while he will tire of it and lie down, but for the time being he acts as if he had been longing, for several hours, to do some smelling and now cannot cover the range of objects fast enough. . . .

The man is also busily employing his sensorial apparatus. He looks. He stands and stares or glances about as he follows the dog. The colors intrigue him. He looks at the new green paint on the benches, at the grass, at the budding trees, at what Wilde termed "that little tent of blue which prisoners call the sky." He has been reading all morning and, in addition to whatever emotional stimulus he gets from the awareness of intake of light, there is pleasure in stretching the complex muscles of his eyes. There is always pleasure in sheer functioning under optimal conditions and he drinks in this pleasure now. Meanwhile, on a more or less subconscious plane of operation, his sight also functions to guide him as he walks. He watches the traffic, he notes the curbs and the obstructions about him. Data furnished by sound, smell, and touch, in addition to those given by sight, he heeds little. They seem not merely of subsidiary importance but of no importance whatever as a contribution to his knowledge of where he is.

His most conscious preoccupation is with the beauty of the scene. Color and degrees of difference in shade certainly create some of this for him. It is useless to enter into the question of whether beauty, or ugliness either, has objective reality; subjective reality they both have. The man is a heliotropic creature. He loves light. Light is associated with well-being, the dark with ill-being. He fears the dark, or at least he fears the need for movement in it. He feels his sight cannot avail him there, but that is not the only reason he distrusts it. He envisions Heaven as filled with light of an immense, perpetual clarity. Dante and Milton have given expression to this belief. Hell is black and gruesome, lighted by cruel fires that only accentuate the dark.

Mythology carries much evidence of symbolism between eye and sun. Horus, god of the sun, had as his symbol the human eye. In the Vedas the sun is called "the eye of the world." Santa Lucia (Holy Light) is the patron saint of eye diseases; she had her martyrdom on the shortest day of the year. The birth of sungods in mythology usually has been associated with the winter solstice.

It is necessary for his well-being that man receive a certain amount of light. So intense is his tropism for light that it is highly probable this has conditioned much of his phylogenetic and cultural development. He has always had a wish to extend himself upward, toward the skies. Maybe this is a wish for God, maybe for the sun; take your choice according to your own lights—and this figure of speech indicates part of our identification of truth with light.

The man, because his sight is the most immediate perceptor of light he has, thinks it is the only receptor of it. His entire organism, however, knows when he has been deprived of light for any length of time. This is more than a matter of feeling mere warmth. His skin is sensitive to it, undergoing change or exposure or removal from it, and reacts in fact to rays the eye cannot perceive. The man's innermost being knows when it is day and when it is night. It is a fable that the blind know the difference between night and day only by the custom by which they live. A vast pulse beat goes through all nature. Vitality rises and falls almost like the tides. Man's stamina is at its lowest in the small hours of morning and his fevers highest at night. The man's certainty that only his eye appreciates light is one of the first overestimations of the role his sight plays in the pattern of his living.

The dog is not so photocentric a creature. In his wild state he is most active at night. His sense of sight, by comparison with man's, is inferior. He is not very good at distinguishing colors. Indeed, whether he can tell the difference among some colors, including red and green, is questionable. It is not true that the Seeing-Eye dog can note the change in traffic lights. But his senses of hearing and smell are very acute. His sense of hearing has been estimated to be sixteen times greater than man's and his olfactory sense so much more acute that calculation of the difference is almost impossible.

The man's superiority over the dog lies in the senses of sight and kinesthesia. Whether the latter in man is actually more acute than it is in the dog is open to question, but it is certainly trained to greater fineness. The man's habit of walking erect keeps him ever on the alert for emergencies. The dog, placed on four legs, has an easier time of it. The man must make finer distinctions in the matter of space and depth and estimate distances more accurately. His binocular vision aids in appreciating depth and perspective. The images from those two cameras, the eyes, fuse and amalgamate by the interlocked distribution system of sight in the brain, to create the impression of one image which, however, has perspective by virtue of the two superimposed images. Man thus adds a further element through his sight to his esthetic system, and in this the distinction in artfulness is made between the photograph and the work of the artist.

All these matters are almost invariably under the control of the involuntary system. The man, however, believes that his conscious will directs them through his eyes. He thinks his sight guards against his falling or stumbling. It seems to be the case with most people that their involuntary attention does assign greater validity to the visual than to the auditory or kinesthetic. Our man, as he goes about, is greatly aided by his hearing in orienting himself, but to the data from hearing he pays little conscious attention. He therefore finds it hard to understand how a man without sight does not stumble more frequently and easily than he does.

The dog's ability to smell is, in the opinion of some observers, and at least under undomestic circumstances, the sense by which he is most quickly made aware of events and objects of interest to him at a distance. It would seem that what the wind carries he can perceive by smell some time before even his keen hearing can catch and classify the information. Both dog and man, then, use the sense which affords each of them the greatest perception of things at a distance as the channel on which they also depend most for stimulation enjoyed for its own sake.

The reception of a stimulus by the retina depends, of course, upon the transmittal to it of light waves. Recent research on the nature of olfaction seems to indicate that this hitherto little understood process also depends upon the reception of radiation of waves, of extremely high frequency, carried by gases. But this is of only minor interest. An esthetic cannot be reasoned out for the dog, even knowing the nature of the sensory process by which he seems to enjoy himself the most, because no one knows what differences, in either kind or degree, he detects in the substances he smells. We do not know, for the most part, what he finds repugnant and what he does not. In the man's case, however, some basis for the knotty problem of esthetics on which philosophers have written tons of books may be worked out in oversimplified form. Colors give pleasure because they are parts of light, components of the spectrum, and are therefore attached to the main body of the stimulating force, namely, light. The ugly is essentially the dark thing, that which is somber, unclear. The dichotomy between good and evil is indicated in the distinction between light and shade. In the well-ordered pattern comprising both, with gradations of color in each, man can see that balance and control between the good and the bad which he seeks perpetually in all living. The feelings of goodness constituted by light he carries over to ideas having nothing to do with seeing. "Light" is an adjective which, as opposed to heavy, indicates that which is capable of rising toward the sky. And in the combination of the two words "heavy" and "dark" the connotation of the ominous, the evil, is carried.

Man consistently makes one mistake in his preoccupation with light. Regarding it as a positive quality, he regards absence of light also as a positive quality, calling it "the dark" and assuming that it actually can be seen. One of the most difficult of all ideas for him to grasp emotionally is that when he "sees" dark he is not seeing it at all but is merely reacting to the absence of light—in other words, that he sees nothing.

One of the remarkable facts connected with this entire situation is that the pain man believes must be caused by the absence of sight he does not also feel to be caused by the absence of hearing. . . .

The power to conceive mentally is so thoroughly equated with visual terms that the language has only the word "imagination" to express it. The word expresses only the idea of picture. If one wishes to speak of conception in terms of touch or hearing, he has to invent phrases such as "auditory imagination" and "tactual imagination." When the art of educating the blind child began to develop, it was found there were no words by which to convey its concepts. These contradictory phrases had to be resorted to. When the phonograph was invented it was found that the language had no word to convey the idea of a captured sound impression in the sense that the words "picture" and "image" indicate a caught sight impression. The inadequate word "record" was selected.

To express comprehension one uses words almost exclusively related to seeing and visualization; he "sees the point," he "views the situation," he "takes a look" or "glances at the evidence." Much less frequently are comprehensive words based on other senses: we do "grasp a problem."

When the evidence of the senses concerning reality conflicts, many will ignore the grossest evidence in favor of what their sight tells them. Witkin and his associates at Brooklyn College showed by carefully controlled experiments that some individuals when sitting in a chair tilted as much as thirty degrees will stubbornly deny the evidence of their sense of balance and believe they are sitting upright because the experimental chamber is designed to convey this visual impression. Witkin also showed that in conflicts between sight and hearing over the origin of sources of sound a surprisingly large number will trust their sight rather than their hearing. An unexplained result of these experiments is that women tend more than men to "believe what they see."

People found it so difficult to believe that the blind child could be educated for the reason that they had to imagine a condition of mind in which, to them, there could be no imagination. Because they could not imagine how understanding in the blind child could develop without imagination, there apparently had to be a "void" in the mind of the blind. When the educability of the blind was demonstrated, theories whereby the other senses transmitted visual impressions were invented to account for it.

Dreams show the extent to which the exercise of the understanding revolves around the visual and the imaginative. Impressions usually interpreted in terms other than sight and even abstractions reduce to pictures. Abstractions, in the dream, never occur as such but condense into pictures, sometimes grotesquely but always possible of reinterpretation in the waking state back to the abstract. A lad dreamed of the abstraction "parents" and saw a composite figure of his father and mother. How sound often translates in the dream into imagery is illustrated by the case of the girl who dreamed of a firecracker going off but instead of hearing the explosion saw the giant word "Bang!" on a great billboard.

Sight comes later than the use of his other senses in the growth of the child. But once it arrives the child begins using it to verify reality as he has learned of it through touch, hearing, and his other senses. It soon seems to assume generalship over the sensorium. The growth of the mental faculties seems to follow this same patterning of events, visualization becoming the focal point for almost all that the adult conceives of as reality. Grasp of reality, or "understanding," becomes identical with visualization. And visualization is shaped by the ability to see. The three become equated, understanding with visualization with sight. Cutting out the middle element, understanding becomes equated with sight.

This equation has bound man to the finite and the material. Because of it he fashioned his very gods after his own image and the images of other creatures he knew. Only the exercise of his highest reason could release him from the equation and show him that what he had conceived of as the unknown was not what he had never seen but that which could not be envisioned. Then, at lengthy and painful last, man knew that what is godlike is that which is beyond the capability of sight ever to capture. . . .

THE DARKNESS CONCEPT

The notion that under blindness there is a constant conscious awareness of absence of light—and therefore an awareness of darkness—has not received much attention from the psychologists, with the exception of Cutsforth. One must begin to examine, with very conscious attention indeed, the language one uses, to note how frequent is reference to the darkness concept. Literature is so deeply imbued with it that it is questionable if the concept can ever be eradicated. There is hardly a book on any phase of the blind problem which is not titled with some variant of the phrase "out of the dark." The senior author's earlier work on blindness inveighed against the concept at some length, yet not only was the review of the books in one of the major New York papers titled "Out of the Darkness" but its text referred twice to "the dark world of the blind."

In speaking of hope in connection with the blind, the word light is used to indicate it. The nation's famous agency is dubbed the Lighthouse. Over the door of the New York Guild for the Jewish Blind appears this sentence: "For all who, in a world of untold beauty, are consigned to darkness, here is light."

Such phrases, except insofar as they tend to reinforce the notion that the blind live in a state of perpetual gloom and melancholy, would probably be little more than euphemistic, did they not do further mischief in suggesting, and so constantly, the void concept. In the effort to imagine what blindness must be like, virtually everyone has, no doubt, at one time or another, shut his eyes. Is it not odd that after having noted the feeling of darkness, those who tried this little experiment did not also note that the feeling of being in the dark passes, after a brief time, to be replaced by the photisms of the imagination? Many blind people do "see" some pervasive color element; usually it is a natural gray but in some it is a constant or intermittent display of what they term "fireworks," which is doubtless due to pathology in the retina. Except for this, what the blind "see" consists of the same photisms of the imagination known to the sighted. "The conclusion that the blind must live in a world of darkness," says Cutsforth,

has been derived through faulty reasoning from Newtonian Physics . . . and if blackness, or darkness, is the opposite of light, then the blind live in a world of complete darkness. The implication is that the blind who so desperately desire to see are confronted, by their inability, with a world of experiential darkness filled with all the horrors of gloom, fear, loneliness, and whatever else the timorous seeing experience in the dark. This is as untrue psychologically as it is physically. . . .

The next passage is from an autobiography written by a young man who, in the spring of 1941, was blinded by a gunshot wound while he was still an undergraduate at Princeton. Here he tells of some of his early attempts to become adjusted to "this foreign setting" after he had begun to recover from his wound and had to face the fact of his blindness.

Cast Off the Darkness

by PETER PUTNAM

My intellectual acceptance of the obvious fact went no further than the statement "I am blind," and the statement had little meaning because it had little application. . . . I was like a traveler who, having missed his ship in some remote port of call, finds that there will not be another one for several weeks or months. There was nothing to do but wait, and while I waited I might as well make myself at home in this foreign setting.

My first and most obvious problem was simply that of finding my way around. In my bedroom, I depended on my hands for orientation. To get to the bathroom, I would feel my way along the length of my bed, take one free-standing step to grope for the corner of the bureau with my left hand, and then pivot around it to reach for the door with my right. Somewhat to my surprise, the stairs were simple. I had to approach them warily, but once I had located the top step, the equal spacing of the treads and the touch of the banister under my hand made descent easy. In the more complicated furniture arrangement of the living room, I used my legs as well as my hands for orientation. The contact of my calves with the seat of a chair was a clue to the direction of the doorway, or my knee brushing the edge of the coffee table made clear the position of the sofa. My most consistent failure was a tendency to overestimate distance. Every room in the house seemed to have shrunk to two-thirds of its former size, and until I had learned to slow and shorten my stride, I was continually barging into things.

I could always ask my family for guidance, but this, too, had its difficulties. It was hard to make verbal instructions precise, and we were amazed at how often we confused left and right when facing each other. On the other hand, to be grabbed by the arms and pushed or pulled in the desired direction was both clumsy and annoying. It was much easier to put my hand on my guide's shoulder and to follow along a little behind and to one side.

Getting around the house was far more awkward than walking outdoors. I recall the first evening my mother and I stepped outside. I kept my hand on her shoulder down the driveway, but after we had turned into the road I let go, and held a parallel course by the sound of her footsteps. There were no distances to gauge and no furniture to bump into, so that I could walk without hesitating and without holding my hands a little in front of me. I was carrying a cane for balance, and as I swung it along beside me, I felt positively jaunty.

There was another reason for my jauntiness that evening, for that was the first time I had got myself fully dressed. After the weeks in pajamas, my clothes seemed coarse and heavy, but I felt stronger and more confident with each item I put on. I can still remember in the minutest detail everything I wore that evening. It was terribly important to me to know exactly how I looked, and this longing for familiarity was accompanied by an exaggerated fastidiousness. The notion that my pants might be baggy, my shoes unshined, or my tie spotted was somehow humiliating, and I took the most elaborate precautions with my appearance. . . .

I tried to discipline my memory and developed a fanatical zeal for neatness, but time and again I would misplace my tie clasp or belt or shoe polish. As I groped through drawers or under the bed, my exasperation mounted steadily, and whenever I was forced to call for help, I was inwardly boiling.

My irritability often turned against others, when their help seemed clumsy or misguided. For example, when I asked where I had put my tie clasp, I meant just that. I wanted to be directed to it, to feel is out myself, and to profit from my mistake. It annoyed me to have it placed in my hand instead. There was some logic in my reasoning, but my irritability was out of all proportion to the occasion, and I cursed myself afterward.

The true source of my impatience with others was my impatience with myself. My efforts to acquire some tolerance for my own blindness were exhausting. I remember the herculean struggles of my

first attempt to change my typewriter ribbon. It took forever, and
I came to hate the cobweb silken softness of the ribbon, which oozed
its ink into my trembling fingers and bent and curled and twisted,
but would not slip into the hair-thin grooves of the ribbon guides
and carrier. Repeatedly I leaned back in my chair to rest, and two
or three times I rose, washed the ink from my sweating hands, and
smoked an entire cigarette, thinking it out in my mind and trying
to sooth the nervousness that made my hands shake and my heart
pound. When it was over at last, I lay down on my bed to listen
to the whole of Beethoven's Seventh.

That summer my records were almost an emotional necessity. It
was a rare day that I did not spend two or three hours listening to
them. They were not simply a means of escape. Apart from the
discipline required to memorize the arrangement of two hundred
records, I was using them as therapy for my frustrations. Whenever
I sensed the approach of one of those fits of nervous exhaustion I
had first noticed in the hospital, I would lie down on my bed and
listen to music until my balance was restored. This was a form of introspection, but it had the affirmative aim of action, for it helped
me to pace myself to my limitations.

In one instance, blindness proved not to be a limitation. About
a month after my first walk, I was coming downstairs into the hall
when some instinct made me jerk back my head. Putting out my
hand, I found that my involuntary movement had saved my fore-
head a nasty bump on the supporting column at the foot of the
staircase.

In a flash, I realized what had happened. Only a few days before,
my sister had read me an article in *Life* on a phenomenon called
"facial vision." Facial vision, it explained, was a faculty developed
by the blind for estimating the distance, direction, and approximate
size of unseen obstacles from the barely audible echoes of incidental
sounds reflecting from them. It is a sort of natural radar in which
footsteps, voices, or even air currents play the part of sound impulses rebounding from opposing surfaces.

I was fascinated by my first experience of it and stood there for
some time, moving my head back and forth beside the column. Each
time I approached, there was a looming sensation, more like feel-

ing than hearing. Later, I found that I could duplicate it by moving my hand toward my ear. I often practiced it sitting in a chair, and when I walked, either indoors or out, I would listen intently for the telltale contraction of echoes when I passed through a doorway or under a tree. I played with my discovery as one might play with a new toy.

As a matter of fact, I played with blindness on a number of levels throughout the summer. One of my most absorbing preoccupations was the exploration of it as a social handicap. With the return of my brother Lo from prep school, my horizons widened. He brought friends to the house and drove me to the houses of other people. Together we took walks, attended the movies, and went to several parties. . . . Lo was not unsympathetic toward my blindness, but he did not seem to be fearful about it. Like me, he viewed it with objective curiosity, investigating its mysteries and experimenting with it in a way that my parents would have found impossible. Many of these experiments were aimless, but they will seem cruel only to those who have forgotten the invulnerability that is also called the indolence, the indifference, and the resilience of youth.

It was inevitably my brother with whom I felt most closely bound in this experimental attitude, but it is clearly illustrated by an incident during a visit from two college classmates, Gordy Bent and Bobby Harvey. They were sitting in my room one morning talking while I dressed, when I noticed an undercurrent of laughter in their conversation.

When I asked what was so funny, their laughter broke into the open.

"It didn't work," Gordy said. "We were trying to fool you."

"We switched your lifeline," Bobby explained, "to see if it wouldn't throw you off, but you've been wandering around for five minutes without making a single mistake."

My "lifeline" was a piece of string tied between my bedpost and the bathroom door. Originally I had used it only to make my way to the lavatory, but they had noticed that I now made frequent contacts with it for purposes of general orientation. Curious to see what would happen, they had transferred one end to another door.

A similar curiosity prompted all sorts of different experiments. While we were taking a walk that same day, Bobby had stopped me, turned me around a few times to confuse my sense of direction, and then asked me to point to where I thought the sun was. Guiding me down a flight of steps, Gordy ducked the shoulder I had my hand on after we had reached the bottom to fool me into taking another downward step. Later in the summer, my brother darted around on the beach to see whether I could follow the sound of his footsteps in the sand, and ran ahead of me, shouting instructions, while I tested my equilibrium on a precarious bicycle ride. There was no immediate purpose to be served by such experiments, but they were useful as explorations of the extent to which my blindness was or was not a handicap.

[In the next section, from an earlier book of Mr. Putnam's, he tells of returning for a football week end at Princeton during the fall following the summer just described.]

The street was Prospect, the town was Princeton, and the excitement which surrounded and warmed me on all sides was that of a gala college football Saturday two hours before game time. . . . We turned off the walk to the right, and Dick's voice cut through my connections with the impersonal crowd and brought me instantly back into contact with my friends.

"Where are we now, Pete?" he asked.

"Easy," I said. "The University Cottage Club." I removed my hand from his shoulder, handed him my cane, and performed a low salaam. They all laughed.

"How'd you know?" Ann asked. "I didn't."

"The brick walk," I kicked my heel against its surface, "portends the 'Brick Shack.' "

"The 'Brick Shack'?"

"The name," I explained, "which the unlettered sometimes apply to the elegant pile before us." Ann laughed cheerfully at almost anything, so I pointed my cane and went on, very pleased with my

From *Keep Your Head Up, Mr. Putnam!* by Peter Putnam. Copyright, 1952, by Peter Putnam. Reprinted by permission of Harper & Brothers.

own success. "Note the classic simplicity of the Georgian style and the geometric effect of the white marble quoins setting off the . . ."

"Cut it out!" Ben said. "I get enough of that stuff in Art 306."

"He's not really blind," Ann said. "He's faking."

"I'm dodging the draft," I said, pleased again. "Once I get a Seeing Eye dog to replace this cane, my disguise will be impenetrable."

"Slacker!" Dick said. "Look out, now! We're coming to the door."

Inside, the clamor of voices engulfed us. As we threaded our way through the standing crowd, there was a shout of "Hi, Pete!" from across the room. I smiled and shouted back, but I did not recognize the voice, and we were headed in the opposite direction.

"Let go of Dick," Ben said, "and give me your other hand."

I did as I was told, and he pulled me through.

"God, what a crush!" I said, "and, boy, how I love it!"

"Here we go," Ben said. "Down these steps."

"Where are you taking me? Don't lock me in the cellar. I want to stay with all the pretty girls."

"All the pretty girls are right behind you," Ann said.

"The alumni had a bar put in the basement this summer," Dick explained. "Wait'll you see it. It's very classy. We're meeting Sandy down there."

I followed Ben down the stairs. We turned left, walked a few paces, and turned again down a longer flight of stairs. At the bottom, we turned right, and I could tell by the sudden contractions of the echoes that we were going through a door. There were many people sitting in this new room, and as we walked, I twisted my body sideways with each rotation of Ben's shoulder to avoid the crowded tables and chairs. I was grateful to Ben for our swift sure passage across the room.

"Hey, group!" Ben called.

The answering shouts came, I guessed, from a table in front of us. I recognized the boys' voices, and I was introduced to two new girls.

"Here's a chair," Dick said, pushing it behind my knees so that I nearly fell into it.

"Easy does it!" I said and reached to my breast pocket for a cigarette. That was something I had gotten into the habit of doing as soon as I came into a new room. It furnished a protective screen of action, behind which I could take my bearings and listen to the relative position of people's voices without seeming to do so. Sandy Prentiss, one of the strange girls and Ben Williamson were on my left. Ann Wylie, Dick Sayer and Dave Compton were on my right. The rest, I decided, were too far away to matter, but I felt a renewed tingle of excitement at the thought that I was back among them.

"Here!" Sandy took my hand and put a drink in it. "Force a little bourbon down your throat."

"Thanks," I said. I took a long drink and settled back as Dick launched into an enthusiastic description of the new bar.

That was how it began, and it seemed like a very fine beginning. We finished our drinks and had another. We talked and laughed in shouts above the clatter of the room, and our conversation was all what we used to call "the old cheap chatter." Dave Compton insisted on taking me up to the bar to test the rail, and when I put my foot on it and called, "Look Ma, no hands," everybody laughed. Everybody laughed at everything. For a while, I rode with the crest of my exhilaration at being back, and the warmth of the whiskey, and the social distinction my blindness gave me, but, then, without any warning, the wave passed over my head and left me floating in its receding wake. I felt tired, removed, a little ashamed of the flush on my face, and, as the remembered sound of my own voice rang in my ears, I was suddenly convinced that my part in the cheap chatter had been really cheap. I had been subject to such emotional oscillations since my blindness and should have been able to guard against them, but Prospect, the club, the girls, the whiskey, and the old friends had been too much for me after the months of absence. I would have to slow down, and I was glad I had arranged to stay in the club instead of going to the game.

"Drink up, everybody!" Dave Compton called. "Let's get this show on the road. If we don't get upstairs and grab some lunch, we'll be late for the kickoff."

"You children toddle on ahead and get your roughage," Sandy

said. "Pete and I are going to have another drink. We never eat
on an empty stomach."

"Are you sure you wouldn't rather go to the game?" I asked.
"You don't have to stay with me, you know. I'd be fine by myself."

"I'd rather hear it on the radio," Sandy said. "I'm too nearsighted
to see anything anyway."

Dick was standing behind my chair.

"We could still get you a ticket if you'd rather go," he said.

"No, this is fine," I said. "I'm kind of tired. I'll meet you here
afterward."

We lingered in the empty bar for a while after the others had
gone, and then Sandy took me upstairs, through the deserted hall
and out onto the terrace court. A lone waiter was noisily piling
plates and glasses upon a metal tray. The surface warmth of the
sun on my face gave me the feeling of the brightness of the day.
Sandy led me forward across the terrace to a comfortably cushioned
cane sofa, and I sat down while he went back inside to get us each
a plate from the buffet. The leatherette of the cushion was warm
against my legs and back. Behind me, in the court, a trickle of
water splashed in the little stone fountain where goldfish were sometimes kept in the spring. Ahead of me, down the slope of the hill,
the muffled voice of the loudspeaker announced the pertinent
statistics of each play, and the occasional roars of the crowd wav-
ered up to me on the soft breath of the cool wind. A fly lit on the
back of my hand, making a tiny spot of cold. Dreamily, I pondered
this for a moment. Maybe the fly's body was itself cold, or, maybe,
even in those few square millimeters of shadow, the absence of the
sun was noticeable on the surface of my skin. I slapped and was
pleased to feel it, for an instant, under my fingers at the moment
of contact, and I remembered, then, that flies got sluggish and easy
to kill in the fall. Sandy came out on the terrace behind me.

"I just killed my first fly in six months," I said.

"Good," Sandy said. "Glad to see you keeping yourself amused.
Here's food."

He set down the plates on a coffee table in front of us. I was
hungry, and I ate with concentration. There was some tomato

aspic that kept falling off my fork, and I was glad there was nobody
but Sandy there to see. I felt relaxed and secure there on the terrace, and I was ready to suggest that Sandy turn on the living-
room radio loud enough so that we could hear it without moving,
but he spoke first.

"Dick tells me you're planning to get a Seeing Eye dog."

"That's right."

"Does that mean there's no more hope for your eyes?"

"I suppose there's always hope for a miracle," I said. "The bullet
hardly touched my eyes at all, but the optic nerves are pretty well
shot. I don't even have light perception. If there were anything left of the nerves, there should have been some sign of it long
ago."

"That's tough."

"I'm lucky I didn't get killed."

Now you should be ready to try an experiment yourself—to
"see" a world without using your eyes. This is an exercise in
sense perception: hearing, smelling, touching, tasting. But it
has a more ambitious purpose too. It suggests, of course, that
the world we think we live in is simply the world we do in fact
perceive and express, in whatever way we do perceive and express it. The world most of us live in, as Chevigny and Braver-
man remind us, is a world lit up, a photocentric existence in
which our very notion of the way we think is told in metaphors
of light. (We see the light at last.) To be blind seems to be one
way of living, often quite satisfactorily, in another sort of world
altogether, where metaphors of light are simply not appropriate.
If all men were blind, the effect on language would be staggering.

DIRECTIONS FOR THEME 2

CHOOSE A PARTICULAR PLACE—THE PLACE OF THEME I OR SOME
OTHER OF YOUR CHOICE—AND BLINDFOLD OR CLOSE YOUR EYES

TIGHTLY FOR AT LEAST TEN OR FIFTEEN MINUTES. THEN WRITE
A DESCRIPTION, AS SENSITIVE AS YOU CAN MAKE IT, OF WHAT
YOU "SAW" UNDER THESE CIRCUMSTANCES, THROUGH YOUR
SENSES OF TOUCH, SMELL, TASTE, AND HEARING. WHAT WOULD
YOU SAY WAS YOUR "POINT OF VIEW" IN THIS COMPOSITION?

3

LEARNING TO SEE

SEE (sī), v. Pa.t. SAW; pa.pple. SEEN. [Com.
Teut.str.vb.; OE.séon. derived from pre-Teut.
sequ-, of disputed relationship.] . . . 3. (fig.)
trans. *To perceive mentally; to apprehend by*
thought (a truth, etc.), to recognize the force
of (a demonstration). Often with ref. to meta-
phorical light or eyes. ME. . . . 4. trans. *With*
mixed literal and fig. sense: To perceive by
visual tokens. ME. b. To learn by reading.
late ME.
—THE SHORTER OXFORD ENGLISH DICTIONARY

Now we are going to read two autobiographical passages in which
men who became particularly skillful at seeing tell how they
learned their art. In the first, a student of the nineteenth-century
scientist, Louis Agassiz, tells how he was taught to see a fish.
This sounds simple, but, as you will discover in his account, it
took Nathaniel Shaler a long time to learn how Agassiz wanted
him to see. The questions we will ask, which Shaler only partially
answers in this passage, are these: Just how does one learn to
see something, besides simply spending a long time at it? Just
what was it Shaler was able to do with his fish, after he had
learned to see it, that he hadn't been able to do before? We

already know that seeing something is more than simply directing one's eyes on it for a period of time. Does Shaler offer any further hints as to what this "more" may be?

Seeing a Fish

by NATHANIEL SOUTHGATE SHALER

At the time of my secession from the humanites, Agassiz was in Europe; he did not return, I think, until the autmun of 1859. I had, however, picked up several acquaintances among his pupils, learned what they were about, and gained some notion of his methods. After about a month he returned, and I had my first contact with the man who was to have the most influence on my life of any of the teachers to whom I am indebted. I shall never forget even the lesser incidents of this meeting, for this great master by his presence gave an importance to his surroundings, so that the room where you met him and the furniture stayed with the memory of him.

When I first met Louis Agassiz, he was still in the prime of his admirable manhood; though he was then fifty-two years old, and had passed his constructive period, he still had the look of a young man. His face was the most genial and engaging that I had ever seen, and his manner captivated me altogether. But as I had been among men who had a free swing, and for a year among people who seemed to me to be cold and super-rational, hungry as I doubtless was for human sympathy, Agassiz's welcome went to my heart —I was at once his captive. It has been my good chance to see many men of engaging presence and ways, but I have never known his equal. . . .

While Agassiz questioned me carefully as to what I had read and what I had seen, he seemed in this preliminary going over in no

From *Autobiography of Nathaniel Southgate Shaler* (Boston: Houghton Mifflin Company, 1907). Reprinted by permission of the estate of Gabriella Shaler Webb.

wise concerned to find what I knew about fossils, rocks, animals, and plants; he put aside the offerings of my scanty lore. This offended me a bit, as I recall, for the reason that I thought I knew, and for a self-taught lad really did know, a good deal about such matters, especially as to the habits of insects, particularly spiders. It seemed hard to be denied the chance to make my parade; but I afterward saw what this meant—that he did not intend to let me begin my tasks by posing as a naturalist. The beginning was indeed quite different, and, as will be seen, in a manner that quickly evaporated my conceit. It was made and continued in a way I will now recount.

Agassiz's laboratory was then in a rather small two-storied building, looking much like a square dwelling-house, which stood where the College Gymnasium now stands . . . Agassiz had recently moved into it from a shed on the marsh near Brighton bridge, the original tenants, the engineers, having come to riches in the shape of the brick structure now known as the Lawrence Building. In this primitive establishment Agassiz's laboratory, as distinguished from the storerooms where the collections were crammed, occupied one room about thirty feet long and fifteen feet wide—what is now the west room on the lower floor of the edifice. In this place, already packed, I had assigned to me a small pine table with a rusty tin pan upon it. . . .

When I sat me down before my tin pan, Agassiz brought me a small fish, placing it before me with the rather stern requirement that I should study it, but should on no account talk to any one concerning it, nor read anything relating to fishes, until I had his permission so to do. To my inquiry, "What shall I do?" he said in effect: "Find out what you can without damaging the specimen; when I think that you have done the work I will question you." In the course of an hour I thought I had compassed that fish; it was rather an unsavory object, giving forth the stench of old alcohol, then loathsome to me, though in time I came to like it. Many of the scales were loosened so that they fell off. It appeared to me to be a case for a summary report, which I was anxious to make and get on to the next stage of the business. But Agassiz, though always within call, concerned himself no further with me that day, nor the next, nor for a week. At first, this neglect was distressing; but

I saw that it was a game, for he was, as I discerned rather than saw, covertly watching me. So I set my wits to work upon the thing, and in the course of a hundred hours or so thought I had done much—a hundred times as much as seemed possible at the start. I got interested in finding out how the scales went in series, their shape, the form and placement of the teeth, etc. Finally, I felt full of the subject, and probably expressed it in my bearing; as for words about it then, there were none from my master except his cheery "Good morning." At length, on the seventh day, came the question, "Well?" and my disgorge of learning to him as he sat on the edge of my table puffing his cigar. At the end of the hour's telling, he swung off and away, saying: "That is not right." Here I began to think that, after all, perhaps the rules for scanning Latin verse were not the worst infliction in the world. Moreover, it was clear that he was playing a game with me to find if I were capable of doing hard, continuous work without the support of a teacher, and this stimulated me to labor. I went at the task anew, discarded my first notes, and in another week of ten hours a day labor I had results which astonished myself and satisfied him. Still there was no trace of praise in words or manner. He signified that it would do by placing before me about a half a peck of bones, telling me to see what I could make of them, with no further directions to guide me. I soon found that they were the skeletons of half a dozen fishes of different species; the jaws told me so much at a first inspection. The task evidently was to fit the separate bones together in their proper order. Two months or more went to this task with no other help than an occasional looking over my grouping with the stereotyped remark: "That is not right." Finally, the task was done, and I was again set upon alcoholic specimens—this time a remarkable lot of specimens representing, perhaps, twenty species of the side-swimmers or Pleuronectidae.

I shall never forget the sense of power in dealing with things which I felt in beginning the more extended work on a group of animals. I had learned the art of comparing objects, which is the basis of the naturalist's work. At this stage I was allowed to read, and to discuss my work with others about me. I did both eagerly, and acquired a considerable knowledge of the literature of ichthyology, becoming especially interested in the system of classification, then most imperfect. I tried to follow Agassiz's scheme of division into the order of ctenoids and ganoids, with the result that I found one of my species of side-swimmers had cycloid scales on one side and ctenoid on the other. This not only shocked my sense of the value of classification in a way that permitted of no full recovery of my original respect for the process, but for a time shook my confidence in my master's knowledge. At the same time I had a malicious pleasure in exhibiting my "find" to him, expecting to repay in part the humiliation which he had evidently tried to inflict on my conceit. To my question as to how the nondescript should be classified he said: "My boy, there are now two of us who know that."

We return to our question: Just how did Shaler learn to see? When Agassiz told him, "That is not right," what did he mean by that? Perhaps if we examine the final paragraph, in which Shaler is describing his "sense of power" *after* he had learned, we can discover something of what his process of learning involved. "I had learned the art of comparing objects," he says. And how does one learn that? There is not much here to go on, but there is at least something in the one example Shaler gives. "I found that one of my species of side-swimmers," he says, "had cycloid scales on one side and ctenoid on the other." Is it possible that one important element in learning to see is the making of distinctions like this one that Shaler "found" between cycloid and ctenoid? Fish scales that were just plain old fish scales before had become differentiated. How? It is a mysterious matter, but this at least we can infer from the evidence Shaler gives us: that whereas at first Shaler was seeing fish scales simply as scales (and "a case for a summary report"), by the end of his learning process he was seeing them as at least two things, cycloid and ctenoid. He had increased his vocabulary. He had gained a "power in dealing with things" which in part at least was a power of language; he had learned to make new distinctions in the classification of fishes by the application of new terms to his experience of seeing.

This process is something like that of reading a difficult passage of literature over and over until you begin to take it in. Shaler learned to "read" his fish—he learned to see words in it, so that what was originally just one more fish in a tray became for him finally a nice intellectual problem suggesting to him the limitations of man-made systems of classifying nature.

This analogy of learning to see with learning to read is made explicit in the next passage you will confront. Here Mark Twain tells how he learned the art of piloting a steamboat on the Mississippi—that is, how he learned to *see* the river. The process of learning to see becomes quite clearly, in Mark Twain's case, a process of "reading" by adding new terms. He looks at the river and he sees a "long slanting line on the face of the water." But this is an inadequate interpretation; it is poor reading. Mr. Bixby, his teacher, translates it for him into pilot-language. "Now, that's a reef. Moreover, it's a bluff reef. There is a solid sand-bar under it that is nearly as straight up and down as the side of a house. . . . If you were to hit it you would knock the boat's brains out." Finally Mark Twain does learn, and the face of the water, he says at the end of our passage, "became a wonderful book—a book that was a dead language to the uneducated passenger, but which told its mind to me without reserve. . . . There never was so wonderful a book written by man. . . ."

That last sentence may be a little ambiguous: Was the book of the river written by man, or not? Evidently not. If it was not written by man, perhaps you might care to ask who it *was* written by.

Seeing the Mississippi

by MARK TWAIN

At the end of what seemed a tedious while, I had managed to pack my head full of islands, towns, bars, "points," and bends; and a curiously inanimate mass of lumber it was, too. However, inasmuch as I could shut my eyes and reel off a good long string of these names without leaving out more than ten miles of river in every fifty, I began to feel that I could take a boat down to New Orleans if I could make her skip those little gaps. But of course my complacency could hardly get start enough to lift my nose a trifle into the air, before Mr. Bixby would think of something to fetch it down again. One day he turned on me suddenly with this settler:

"What is the shape of Walnut Bend?"

He might as well have asked me my grandmother's opinion of protoplasm. I reflected respectfully, and then said I didn't know it had any particular shape. My gun-powdery chief went off with a bang, of course, and then went on loading and firing until he was out of adjectives.

I had learned long ago that he only carried just so many rounds of ammunition, and was sure to subside into a very placable and even remorseful old smoothbore as soon as they were all gone. That word "old" is merely affectionate; he was not more than thirty-four. I waited. By and by he said:

"My boy, you've got to know the *shape* of the river perfectly. It is all there is left to steer by on a very dark night. Everything else is blotted out and gone. But mind you, it hasn't the same shape in the night that it has in the daytime."

"How on earth am I ever going to learn it, then?"

"How do you follow a hall at home in the dark? Because you know the shape of it. You can't see it."

"Do you mean to say that I've got to know all the million trifling

From *Life on the Mississippi* (1883).

variations of shape in the banks of this interminable river as well as I know the shape of the front hall at home?"

"On my honor, you've got to know them *better* than any man ever did know the shapes of the halls in his own house."

"I wish I was dead!"

"Now I don't want to discourage you, but—"

"Well, pile it on me; I might as well have it now as another time."

"You see, this has got to be learned; there isn't any getting around it. A clear starlight night throws such heavy shadows that, if you didn't know the shape of a shore perfectly, you would claw away from every bunch of timber, because you would take the black shadow of it for a solid cape; and you see you would be getting scared to death every fifteen minutes by the watch. You would be fifty yards from shore all the time when you ought to be within fifty feet of it. You can't see a snag in one of those shadows, but you know exactly where it is, and the shape of the river tells you when you are coming to it. Then there's your pitch-dark night; the river is a very different shape on a pitch-dark night from what it is on a star-light night. All shores seem to be straight lines, then, and mighty dim ones, too; and you'd *run* them for straight lines, only you know better. You boldly drive your boat right into what seems to be a solid, straight wall (you knowing very well that in reality there is a curve there), and that wall falls back and makes way for you. Then there's your gray mist. You take a night when there's one of these grisly, drizzly, gray mists, and then there isn't *any* particular shape to a shore. A gray mist would tangle the head of the oldest man that ever lived. Well, then, different kinds of *moonlight* change the shape of the river in different ways. You see—"

"Oh, don't say any more, please! Have I got to learn the shape of the river according to all these five hundred thousand different ways? If I tried to carry all that cargo in my head it would make me stoop-shouldered."

"*No!* you only learn *the* shape of the river; and you learn it with such absolute certainty that you can always steer by the shape that's *in your head,* and never mind the one that's before your eyes."

"Very well, I'll try it; but, after I have learned it, can I depend on it? Will it keep the same form and not go fooling around?"

Before Mr. Bixby could answer, Mr. W. came in to take the watch, and he said:

"Bixby, you'll have to look out for President's Island, and all that country clear away up above the Old Hen and Chickens. The banks are caving and the shape of the shores changing like everything. Why, you wouldn't know the point above 40. You can go up inside the old sycamore snag, now."

So that question was answered. Here were leagues of shore changing shape. My spirits were down in the mud again. Two things seemed pretty apparent to me. One was, that in order to be a pilot a man had got to learn more than any one man ought to be allowed to know; and the other was, that he must learn it all over again in a different way every twenty-four hours. . . .

It was plain that I had got to learn the shape of the river in all the different ways that could be thought of—upside down, wrong end first, inside out, fore-and-aft, and "thort-ships"—and then know what to do on gray nights when it hadn't any shape at all. So I set about it. In the course of time I began to get the best of this knotty lesson, and my self-complacency moved to the front once more. Mr. Bixby was all fixed, and ready to start it to the rear again. He opened on me after this fashion:

"How much water did we have in the middle crossing at Hole-in-the-Wall, trip before last?"

I considered this an outrage. I said:

"Every trip, down and up, the leadsmen are singing through that tangled place for three-quarters of an hour on a stretch. How do you reckon I can remember such a mess as that?"

"My boy, you've got to remember it. You've got to remember the exact spot and the exact marks the boat lay in when we had the shoalest water, in every one of the five hundred shoal places between St. Louis and New Orleans; and you mustn't get the shoal soundings and marks of one trip mixed up with the shoal soundings and marks of another, either, for they're not often twice alike. You must keep them separate."

When I came to myself again, I said:

"When I get so that I can do that, I'll be able to raise the dead, and then I won't have to pilot a steamboat to make a living. I want to retire from this business. I want a slush-bucket and a brush; I'm only fit for a roustabout. I haven't got brains enough to be a pilot; and if I had I wouldn't have strength enough to carry them around, unless I went on crutches."

"Now drop that! When I say I'll learn * a man the river, I mean it. And you can depend on it, I'll learn him or kill him."

.   .   .

There was no use in arguing with a person like this. I promptly put such a strain on my memory that by and by even the shoal water and the countless crossing-marks began to stay with me. But the result was just the same. I never could more than get one knotty thing learned before another presented itself. Now I had often seen pilots gazing at the water and pretending to read it as if it were a book; but it was a book that told me nothing. A time came at last, however, when Mr. Bixby seemed to think me far enough advanced to bear a lesson on water-reading. So he began:

"Do you see that long, slanting line on the face of the water? Now, that's a reef. Moreover, it's a bluff reef. There is a solid sand-bar under it that is nearly as straight up and down as the side of a house. There is plenty of water close up to it, but mighty little on top of it. If you were to hit it you would knock the boat's brains out. Do you see where the line fringes out at the upper end and begins to fade away?"

"Yes, sir."

"Well, that is a low place; that is the head of the reef. You can climb over there, and not hurt anything. Cross over, now, and follow along close under the reef—easy water there—not much current."

I followed the reef along till I approached the fringed end. Then Mr. Bixby said:

"Now get ready. Wait till I give the word. She won't want to mount the reef; a boat hates shoal water. Stand by—wait—*wait*—

* "Teach" is not in the river vocabulary.

keep her well in hand. *Now* cramp her down! Snatch her! snatch her!"

He seized the other side of the wheel and helped to spin it around until it was hard down, and then we held it so. The boat resisted, and refused to answer for a while, and next she came surging to starboard, mounted the reef, and sent a long, angry ridge of water foaming away from her bows.

"Now watch her; watch her like a cat, or she'll get away from you. When she fights strong and the tiller slips a little, in a jerky, greasy sort of way, let up on her a trifle; it is the way she tells you at night that the water is too shoal; but keep edging her up, little by little, toward the point. You are well up on the bar now; there is a bar under every point, because the water that comes down around it forms an eddy and allows the sediment to sink. Do you see those fine lines on the face of the water that branch out like the ribs of a fan? Well, those are little reefs; you want to just miss the ends of them, but run them pretty close. Now look out—look out! Don't you crowd that slick, greasy-looking place; there ain't nine feet there; she won't stand it. She begins to smell it; look sharp, I tell you! Oh, blazes, there you go! Stop the starboard wheel! Quick! Ship up to back! Set her back!"

The engine bells jingled and the engines answered promptly, shooting white columns of steam far aloft out of the 'scape-pipes, but it was too late. The boat had "smelt" the bar in good earnest; the foamy ridges that radiated from her bows suddenly disappeared, a great dead swell came rolling forward, and swept ahead of her, she careened far over to larboard, and went tearing away toward the shore as if she were about scared to death. We were a good mile from where we ought to have been when we finally got the upper hand of her again.

During the afternoon watch the next day, Mr. Bixby asked me if I knew how to run the next few miles. I said:

"Go inside the first snag above the point, outside the next one, start out from the lower end of Higgins's woodyard, make a square crossing, and—"

"That's all right. I'll be back before you close up on the next point."

But he wasn't. He was still below when I rounded it and entered upon a piece of the river which I had some misgivings about. I did not know that he was hiding behind a chimney to see how I would perform. I went gaily along, getting prouder and prouder, for he had never left the boat in my sole charge such a length of time before. I even got to "setting" her and letting the wheel go entirely, while I vaingloriously turned my back and inspected the stern marks and hummed a tune, a sort of easy indifference which I had prodigiously admired in Bixby and other great pilots. Once I inspected rather long, and when I faced to the front again my heart flew into my mouth so suddenly that if I hadn't clapped my teeth together I should have lost it. One of those frightful bluff reefs was stretching its deadly length right across our bows! My head was gone in a moment; I did not know which end I stood on; I gasped and could not get my breath; I spun the wheel down with such rapidity that it wove itself together like a spider's web; the boat answered and turned square away from the reef, but the reef followed her! I fled, but still it followed, still it kept—right across my bows! I never looked to see where I was going, I only fled. The awful crash was imminent. Why didn't that villain come? If I committed the crime of ringing a bell I might get thrown overboard. But better that than kill the boat. So in blind desperation, I started such a rattling "shivaree" down below as never had astounded an engineer in this world before, I fancy. Amidst the frenzy of the bells the engines began to back and fill in a curious way, and my reason forsook its throne—we were about to crash into the woods on the other side of the river. Just then Mr. Bixby stepped calmly into view on the hurricane-deck. My soul went out to him in gratitude. My distress vanished; I would have felt safe on the brink of Niagara with Mr. Bixby on the hurricane-deck. He blandly and sweetly took his toothpick out of his mouth between his fingers, as if it were a cigar—we were just in the act of climbing an overhanging big tree, and the passengers were scudding astern like rats— and lifted up these commands to me ever so gently:

"Stop the starboard! Stop the larboard! Set her back on both!"

The boat hesitated, halted, pressed her nose among the boughs a critical instant, then reluctantly began to back away.

"Stop the larboard! Come ahead on it! Stop the starboard! Come ahead on it! Point her for the bar!"

I sailed away as serenely as a summer's morning. Mr. Bixby came in and said, with mock simplicity:

"When you have a hail, my boy, you ought to tap the big bell three times before you land, so that the engineers can get ready."

I blushed under the sarcasm, and said I hadn't had any hail.

"Ah! Then it was for wood, I suppose. The officer of the watch will tell you when he wants to wood up."

I went on consuming, and said I wasn't after wood.

"Indeed? Why, what could you want over here in the bend, then? Did you ever know of a boat following a bend up-stream at this stage of the river?"

"No, sir—and *I* wasn't trying to follow it. I was getting away from a bluff reef."

"No, it wasn't a bluff reef; there isn't one within three miles of where you were."

"But I saw it. It was as bluff as that one yonder."

"Just about. Run over it!"

"Do you give it as an order?"

"Yes. Run over it!"

"If I don't, I wish I may die."

"All right; I am taking the responsibility."

I was just as anxious to kill the boat, now, as I had been to save it before. I impressed my orders upon my memory, to be used at the inquest, and made a straight break for the reef. As it disappeared under our bows I held my breath; but we slid over it like oil.

"Now, don't you see the difference? It wasn't anything but a *wind* reef. The wind does that."

"So I see. But it is exactly like a bluff reef. How am I ever going to tell them apart?"

"I can't tell you. It is an instinct. By and by you will just naturally *know* one from the other, but you never will be able to explain why or how you know them apart."

It turned out to be true. The face of the water, in time, became a wonderful book—a book that was a dead language to the uneducated passenger, but which told its mind to me without reserve, delivering its most cherished secrets as clearly as if it uttered them with a voice. And it was not a book to be read once and thrown aside, for it had a new story to tell every day. Throughout the long twelve hundred miles there was never a page that was void of interest, never one that you could leave unread without loss, never one that you would want to skip, thinking you could find higher enjoyment in some other thing. There never was so wonderful a book written by man; never one whose interest was so absorbing, so unflagging, so sparklingly renewed with every reperusal. The passenger who could not read it was charmed with a peculiar sort of faint dimple on its surface (on the rare occasions when he did not overlook it altogether); but to the pilot that was an *italicized* passage; indeed, it was more than that, it was a legend of the largest capitals, with a string of shouting exclamation-points at the end of it, for it meant that a wreck or a rock was buried there that could tear the life out of the strongest vessel that ever floated. It is the faintest and simplest expression the water ever makes, and the most hideous to a pilot's eye. In truth, the passenger who could not read this book saw nothing but all manner of pretty pictures in it, painted by the sun and shaded by the clouds, whereas to the trained eye these were not pictures at all, but the grimmest and most dead-earnest of reading-matter.

Scholars of American literature have pointed out that the way Mark Twain described himself as a young man in *Life on the Mississippi* and other "autobiographical" works was decidedly fictitious.* The fact is, they say, Mark Twain early in life knew a lot about the river, and he was never the ignorant fool he later made himself out to be. Would you say that therefore Mark Twain was a liar? Maybe so, but a more sensible remark might be that it suited the writer's purpose to recollect himself in this

* See, for example, Henry Nash Smith, "Mark Twain as an Interpreter of the Far West: The Structure of *Roughing It*," in *The Frontier in Perspective*, eds. Walker D. Wyman and Clifton B. Kroeber (Madison: The University of Wisconsin Press, 1957).

way, perhaps because the experience of learning to "read" the river becomes more dramatic and amusing if the learner is a foolish innocent. The "I" of the passage we have just read is a *character* in the story, and in this case he apparently bore very little relation to the real-life author who created him.

This suggests still another meaning for our complex phrase, point of view. Part of the point from which you view something is the character of the viewer, the "I" of your story. Naturally you want to make this "I" as true to the experience you are describing as you can. Yet, as we have already said, you can hardly do justice in any case to the richness and variety of your real self at any given moment—much less a moment that happened perhaps years ago. Inevitably you must select, ruling out some things and filling in others with whatever your imagination and your sense of your final purpose can provide. Inevitably you become a character in your own story. You have made yourself over, perhaps not as drastically as Mark Twain did, but certainly somewhat.

Now to our next job of writing. The languages of the biologist or the river pilot may seem remote to you. But you have some languages of your own: you too "read" the world around you all the time, and some of your reading is very skillful. For example, you may have learned enough about baseball to "read" the way a batter holds his feet as an indication that he may be a sucker for an outside curve, or may be ready to bunt, or whatever. Many people have learned enough about hunting to "read" animal tracks in the woods—a language with hundreds of words in it. Perhaps you know something of an auto mechanic's language, and can "read" certain engine noises as symptomatic of this or that impending disaster. Whatever it is that you know (and it is surely something), this exercise asks you to look at it carefully and tell your reader about an example of your learning.

DIRECTIONS FOR THEME 3

CHOOSE A PARTICULAR AREA OF YOUR KNOWLEDGE, AND DE-
SCRIBE IN DETAIL A PARTICULAR EXPERIENCE IN WHICH YOU
LEARNED TO "READ." TELL THE CIRCUMSTANCES: WHERE YOU
WERE, WHAT YOU WERE TRYING TO DO, WHO TAUGHT YOU, WHAT
IT WAS YOU LEARNED. AT THE END OF YOUR THEME, SAY JUST
WHAT YOU MEAN BY "LEARNING" IN THE CONTEXT OF THIS EX-
PERIENCE.

4

SEEING A FAMILY CONFLICT

I began to wonder at about this time just what one saw when one looked at anything really looked at anything.

—GERTRUDE STEIN

You have now confronted three varied problems associated with acts of seeing.

In Theme 1 you described a simple visual experience that you had. For you as a writer, this activity of "seeing" became a matter of selection, a matter of words chosen as best you could to achieve a desired result. You started with what you saw, with your eyes, but you ended with what you *said* you saw, from a chosen point of view, and that was a far different thing from your primary experience. It was more controlled and organized; it was also, as against the chaotic fullness of the original experience, more limited.

In Theme 2 you were cut off altogether from visual experience, yet your problem as a writer was the same. Out of the rich blur of sensation that you felt when blindfolded, you selected what you could to put in words. "I see, said the blind man" is an old joke, but we can understand now that it is more than a joke. It suggests that seeing is necessarily bound up with mental activities of interpreting and selecting and expressing. In that sense a blind man can see as well as you and I—and seeing is at the very center of the writer's situation.

You developed this implication in Theme 3, where you treated seeing as a kind of "reading." Objects you perceived, whether with your eyes or your ears or some other medium of awareness, became symbols that you could translate meaningfully into some other terms for your own use and the use of others. These terms were the words used in a particular kind of activity, such as baseball, hunting, auto mechanics—activities where such discriminations have to be made if the job is to be done.

Now we are going to have a look at another sort of experience out of your own recent past. This is the experience of family conflict, a subject in which we can all probably claim some *expertise*. Consider all the times you have wanted something and couldn't have it because of the opposition of your parents. How would you *see* such an experience? What position, what point of view, would be proper and convincing for you to adopt? Whose side should you favor and whose oppose? These are some of the questions you must answer in writing Theme 4.

First, however, we shall read a passage from a famous American novel of a generation ago, a passage in which a kind of classic family conflict takes place. Here Mr. George F. Babbitt, whose name has become synonymous with a satirical version of the American business man, faces breakfast with his family.

Breakfast at the Babbitts'

by SINCLAIR LEWIS

Often of a morning Babbitt came bouncing and jesting in to breakfast. But things were mysteriously awry to-day. As he pontifically tread the upper hall he looked into Verona's bedroom and protested, "What's the use of giving the family a high-class house when they don't appreciate it and tend to business and get down to brass tacks?"

He marched upon them: Verona, a dumpy brown-haired girl of twenty-two, just out of Bryn Mawr, given to solicitudes about duty and sex and God and the unconquerable bagginess of the gray sports-suit she was now wearing. Ted—Theodore Roosevelt Babbitt —a decorative boy of seventeen. Tinka—Katherine—still a baby at ten, with radiant red hair and a thin skin which hinted of too much candy and too many ice cream sodas. Babbitt did not show his vague irritation as he tramped in. He really disliked being a family tyrant, and his nagging was as meaningless as it was frequent. He shouted at Tinka, "Well, kittiedoolie!" It was the only pet name in his vocabulary, except the "dear" and "hon." with which he recognized his wife, and he flung it at Tinka every morning.

He gulped a cup of coffee in the hope of pacifying his stomach and his soul. His stomach ceased to feel as though it did not belong to him, but Verona began to be conscientious and annoying, and abruptly there returned to Babbitt the doubts regarding life and families and business which had clawed at him when his dream-life . . . had fled.

Verona had for six months been filing-clerk at the Gruensberg Leather Company offices, with a prospect of becoming secretary to Mr. Gruensberg and thus, as Babbitt defined it, "getting some good out of your expensive college education till you're ready to marry and settle down."

But now said Verona: "Father! I was talking to a classmate of mine that's working for the Associated Charities—oh, Dad, there's the sweetest little babies that come to the milkstation there!—and I feel as though I ought to be doing something worth while like that."

"What do you mean 'worth while'? If you get to be Gruensberg's secretary—and maybe you would, if you kept up your shorthand and didn't go sneaking off to concerts and talkfests every evening— I guess you'll find thirty-five or forty bones a week worth while!"

"I know, but—oh, I want to—contribute— I wish I were working in a settlement-house. I wonder if I could get one of the depart-ment-stores to let me put in a welfare-department with a nice rest-room and chintzes and wicker chairs and so on and so forth. Or I could—"

"Now you look here! The first thing you got to understand is that all this uplift and flipflop and settlement-work and recreation is nothing in God's world but the entering wedge for socialism. The sooner a man learns he isn't going to be coddled, and he needn't expect a lot of free grub and, uh, all these free classes and flipflop and doodads for his kids unless he earns 'em, why, the sooner he'll get on the job and produce—produce—produce! That's what the country needs, and not all this fancy stuff that just enfeebles the will-power of the working man and gives his kids a lot of notions above their class. And you—if you'd tend to business instead of fooling and fussing— All the time! When I was a young man I made up my mind what I wanted to do, and stuck to it through thick and thin, and that's why I'm where I am to-day, and— Myra! What do you let the girl chop the toast up into these dinky little chunks for? Can't get your fist onto'em. Half cold, anyway!"

Ted Babbitt, junior in the great East Side High School, had been making hiccup-like sounds of interruption. He blurted now, "Say, Rone, you going to—"

Verona whirled. "Ted! Will you kindly not interrupt us when we're talking about serious matters!"

"Aw, punk," said Ted judicially. "Ever since somebody slipped up and let you out of college, Ammonia, you been pulling these nut conversations about what-nots and so-on-and-so-forths. Are you going to— I want to use the car tonight."

Babbitt snorted, "Oh, you do! May want it myself!" Verona protested, "Oh, you do, Mr. Smarty! I'm going to take it myself!" Tinka wailed, "Oh papa, you said maybe you'd drive us down to Rosedale!" and Mrs. Babbitt, "Careful, Tinka, your sleeve is in the butter." They glared, and Verona hurled, "Ted, you're a perfect pig about the car!"

"Course you're not! Not a-tall!" Ted could be maddeningly bland. "You just want to grab it off, right after dinner, and leave it in front of some skirt's house all evening while you sit and gas about lite'ature and the highbrows you're going to marry—if they only propose!"

"Well, Dad oughtn't to *ever* let you have it! You and those beastly Jones boys drive like maniacs. The idea of your taking the turn on Chautauqua Place at forty miles an hour!"

"Aw, where do you get that stuff! You're so darn scared of the car that you drive up-hill with the emergency brake on!"

"I do not! And you— Always talking about how much you know about motors, and Eunice Littlefield told me you said the battery fed the generator!"

"You—why, my good woman, you don't know a generator from a differential." Not unreasonably was Ted lofty with her. He was a natural mechanic, a maker and tinkerer of machines; he lisped in blueprints for the blueprints came.

"That'll do now!" Babbitt flung in mechanically, as he lighted the gloriously satisfying first cigar of the day and tasted the exhilarating drug of the *Advocate-Times* headlines.

Ted negotiated: "Gee, honest, Rone, I don't want to take the old boat, but I promised couple o' girls in my class I'd drive 'em down to the rehearsal of the school chorus, and, gee, I don't want to, but a gentleman's got to keep his social engagements."

"Well, upon my word! You and your social engagements! In high school!"

"Oh, ain't we select since we went to that hen college! Let me tell you there isn't a private school in the state that's got as swell a bunch as we got in Gamma Digamma this year. There's two fellows that their dads are millionaires. Say, gee, I ought to have a car of my own, like lots of the fellows."

Babbitt almost rose. "A car of your own! Don't you want a yacht, and a house and lot? That pretty nearly takes the cake! A boy that can't pass his Latin examinations, like any other boy ought to, and he expects me to give him a motor-car, and I suppose a chauffeur, and an aero-plane maybe, as a reward for the hard work he puts in going to the movies with Eunice Littlefield! Well, when you see me giving you—"

Somewhat later, after diplomacies, Ted persuaded Verona to admit that she was merely going to the Armory, that evening, to see the dog and cat show. She was then, Ted planned, to park the car in front of the candy-store across from the Armory and he would pick it up. There were masterly arrangements regarding leaving the key, and having the gasoline tank filled; and passionately, devotees of the Great God Motor, they hymned the patch on the spare inner-tube, and the lost jackhandle.

Their truce dissolving, Ted observed that her friends were "a scream of a bunch—stuck-up gabby four-flushers." His friends, she indicated, were "disgusting imitation sports, and horrid little shrieking ignorant girls." Further: "It's disgusting of you to smoke cigarettes, and so on and so forth, and those clothes you've got on this morning, they're too utterly ridiculous—honestly, simply disgusting."

Ted balanced over to the low beveled mirror in the buffet, regarded his charms, and smirked. His suit, the latest thing in Old Eli Togs, was skin-tight, with skimpy trousers to the tops of his glaring tan boots, a chorus-man waistline, pattern of an agitated check, and across the back a belt which belted nothing. His scarf was an enormous black silk wad. His flaxen hair was ice-smooth, pasted back without parting. When he went to school he would add a cap with a long vizor like a shovel-blade. Proudest of all was his waistcoat, saved for, begged for, plotted for; a real Fancy Vest of fawn with polka dots of a decayed red, the points astoundingly long. On the lower edge of it he wore a high-school button, a class button, and a fraternity pin.

And none of it mattered. He was supple and swift and flushed;

his eyes (which he believed to be cynical) were candidly eager. But he was not over-gentle. He waved his hand at poor dumpy Verona and drawled: "Yes, I guess we're pretty ridiculous and disgusticulus, and I rather guess our new necktie is some smear!"

Babbitt barked: "It is! And while you're admiring yourself, let me tell you it might add to your manly beauty if you wiped some of that egg off your mouth!"

Verona giggled, momentary victor in the greatest of Great Wars, which is the family war. Ted looked at her hopelessly, then shrieked at Tinka: "For the love o' Pete, quit pouring the whole sugar bowl on your corn flakes!"

When Verona and Ted were gone and Tinka upstairs, Babbitt groaned to his wife: "Nice family, I must say! I don't pretend to be any baa-lamb, and maybe I'm a little cross-grained at breakfast sometimes, but the way they go on jab-jab-jabbering, I simply can't stand it. I swear, I feel like going off some place where I can get a little peace. I do think after a man's spent his lifetime trying to give his kids a chance and a decent education, it's pretty discouraging to hear them all the time scrapping like a bunch of hyenas and never—and never— Curious; here in the paper it says— Never silent for one mom— Seen the morning paper yet?"

"No, dear." In twenty-three years of married life, Mrs. Babbitt had seen the paper before her husband just sixty-seven times.

"Lots of news. Terrible big tornado in the South. Hard luck, all right. But this, say, this is corking! Beginning of the end for those fellows! New York Assembly has passed some bills that ought to completely outlaw the socialists! And there's an elevator-runners' strike in New York and a lot of college boys are taking their places. That's the stuff! And a mass-meeting in Birmingham's demanded that this Mick agitator, this fellow De Valera, be deported. Dead right, by golly! All these agitators paid with German gold anyway. And we got no business interfering with the Irish or any other foreign government. Keep our hands strictly off. And there's another well-authenticated rumor from Russia that Lenin is dead. That's fine. It's beyond me why we don't just step in there and kick those Bolshevik cusses out."

"That's so," said Mrs. Babbitt.

The writing here is perhaps a little more complicated than it looks. The point of view, the position the narrator adopts, seems at first to be that of Babbitt himself. Notice how, in the third paragraph, the narrator tells us things that he could know only if he were "inside" Babbitt, such as what his hopes were as he gulped his coffee, how his stomach felt, what doubts returned to his mind. This is the sort of information we never have about other people except in literature. (In ordinary life we have to guess at what other people may be thinking.) And even in literature there are limits. It is customary for a narrator in a story or novel to presume to know the inside of only one character at a time; usually, having taken one person's point of view, he sticks to that one and does not flit about from one mind to another. There are plenty of exceptions to this rule, and even in the short passage you have just read there is some shifting of the narrator's intimacy, though it is not abrupt. (Thus, on page 51, the narrator tells us some of the secret thoughts of Ted—that he believes his eyes look romantically cynical, for instance.) Nevertheless, the position the narrator seems to adopt, as he follows Babbitt downstairs to the breakfast table and through the meal, is that of poor old Babbitt himself.

But this is obviously only a superficial account of the total point of view we encounter here. It is true that we follow Babbitt down the upper hall like a camera on a dolly, and we are told to some extent what he is thinking, but the attitudes or value judgments we are invited to accept toward the scene are definitely not his. "He marched upon them"—already we sense the ludicrous in Babbitt. Are we on his side in the family conflict? Hardly. When he answers his daughter's sentiments about settlement work with the lecture on uplift and flipflop ("produce—produce—produce"), clearly we are expected to jeer at him. When he answers his son's appeal for a car of his own, we recognize the conventional language of paternal hysteria, and we smile. On the other hand it does not follow that therefore we admire Verona's senti' mental uplift or that we support Ted's appeal for another car. It may be that we are rather against everybody in this little breakfast scene, and it may even be that this writing is pretty cruel.

In your own theme on this subject you can be cruel or charitable, just as you wish—but one of your protagonists, an important one, is yourself.

DIRECTIONS FOR THEME 4

DESCRIBE A CONFLICT BETWEEN YOURSELF AND ONE OR BOTH OF YOUR PARENTS. DRAMATIZE THIS CONFLICT BY MEANS OF A PARTICULAR INCIDENT IN WHICH YOU SHOW AS VIVIDLY AS YOU CAN JUST WHAT PEOPLE SAID AND DID ON THIS OCCASION.

In one way or another, the point of view you take in Theme 4 will of course be your own: this is autobiography, and you are seeing life through your own remembering eyes. You may be able to use language so skillfully as to lead your reader to adopt a final attitude or judgment on the conflict that will be other than the one you held at the time. But be careful to keep your narrator's location in the scene within yourself. You are the only character in your drama whose thoughts and emotions you can presume to express. Express them.

THEME

5

CONFLICT AS ANTHROPOLOGY

No man ever looks at the world with pristine eyes. He sees it edited by a definite set of customs and institutions and ways of thinking.
—RUTH BENEDICT

Now you are going to be asked to change your point of view toward your conflict of Theme 4 by seeing it again in another light.

What *is* "another light"?—and note that photocentric metaphor. Another light, to put it at its simplest, is another way of talking, another way of "reading" in the sense of Theme 3. And how can you acquire another way of talking? One way, obviously, is by learning new words. And you learn new words by listening, by reading books—in fact, by going to college. One could call a college education an introduction to various ways of useful talking, and it is in that sense that this book seeks to expose you to some changes in the ways you see things, the ways you talk about them.

For our immediate purpose, the reseeing of a family conflict in new terms, we need a piece of writing that will provide us with some new terms for possible use. The passage that follows is by a famous anthropologist, and it employs certain words and phrases that are characteristic of an anthropologist's particular activity. As you read this article, try to stay alert for words and phrases (new terms) that might help you see your situation of Theme 4 in some fresh way. How much, if any, of this passage can you make relevant to yourself and your conflict?

The Mock Battle in the American Family

by MARGARET MEAD

Educators exclaim impatiently over the paradox that Americans believe in change, believe in progress and yet do their best—or so it seems—to retard their children, to bind them to parental ways, to inoculate them against the new ways to which they give lip service. But here is a point where the proof of the pudding lies in the eating. If the parents were really behaving as the impatient educators claim they are, really strangling and hobbling their children's attempts to embrace the changing fashions in manners or morals, we would not have the rapid social change which is so characteristic of our modern life. We would not go in twenty years from fig leaves on Greek statues to models of unborn babies in our public museums. It is necessary to distinguish between ritual and ceremonial resistances and real resistances. Among primitive peoples, we find those in which generation after generation there is a mock battle between the young men and the old men: generation after generation the old men lose. An observer from our society, with an unresolved conflict with his father on his mind, might watch that battle in terror, feeling the outcome was in doubt. But the members of the tribe who are fighting the mock battle consciously or unconsciously know the outcome and fight with no less display of zeal for the knowing of it. The mock battle is no less important because the issue is certain.

Similarly, on the island of Bali, it is unthinkable that a father or a brother should plan to give a daughter of the house to some outsider. Only when a marriage is arranged between cousins, both of whose fathers are members of the same paternal line, can consent be appropriately given. Yet there flourishes, and has flourished probably for hundreds of years, a notion among Balinese young people that it is more fun to marry someone who is not a cousin. So, generation after generation, young men carry off the daughters of other men, and these daughters, their consent given in advance, nevertheless shriek and protest noisily if there are witnesses by. It is a staged abduction, in which no one believes, neither the boy nor the girl nor their relatives. Once in a while, some neurotic youth misunderstands and tries to abduct a girl who has not given her consent, and as a result the whole society is plunged into endless confusion, recrimination, and litigation.

So it is in American society. American parents, to the extent that they are Americans, expect their children to live in a different world, to clothe their moral ideas in different trappings, to court in automobiles although their forebears courted, with an equal sense of excitement and moral trepidation, on horsehair sofas. As the parents' course was uncharted when they were young—for they too had gone a step beyond their parents and transgressed every day some boundary which their parents had temporarily accepted as absolute—so also the parents know that their children are sailing uncharted seas. And so it comes about that American parents lack the sure hand on the rudder which parents in other societies display, and that they go in for a great deal of conventional and superficial grumbling. To the traditional attitudes characteristic of all oldsters who find the young a deteriorated version of themselves, Americans add the mixture of hope and envy and anxiety which comes from knowing that their children are not deteriorated versions of themselves, but actually—very actually—manage a car better than father ever did. This is trying; sometimes very trying. The neurotic father, like the neurotic lover in Bali, will misunderstand the license to grumble, and will make such a fuss over his son or daughter when they behave as all of their age are behaving, that the son or daughter has to be very unneurotic indeed not to take the fuss as something serious, not to believe that he or she is breaking father's heart. Similarly, a neurotic son or daughter will mistake the ceremonial grumbling for the real thing, and break their spirits in a futile attempt to live up to the voiced parental standards. To the average child the parents' resistance is a stimulus.

On the east coast, people grumble about the coming of winter, lament over the wild geranium which marks the end of spring, and shudder noisily away from the winter that they would not do without. Occasionally, someone takes this seasonal grumbling seriously and moves to Southern California; but for most people, born and bred in a north temperate climate, the zest and tang of the too cold winter is as essential a part of life as the sultry heat and wilting flowers of the too hot summer. If one were to do a series of interviews among immigrants to Southern California, one would go away convinced that Americans had but one aim, to escape from the dreadful rigors of the north temperate zone into the endless health-giving, but eventless balminess, of a Riviera climate. This would be quite wrong. It would be equally wrong to suppose the Southern Californian insincere in his passionate climatophilism. Just as the flight from the bruising effects of winter to the soothing effects of no winter at all is a part of the American scene, so each generation of Americans produces a certain number of fathers and sons who make personal tragedies out of the changing character of the American scene; tragedies which have their own language, music and folklore, and are an inalienable part of that American scene.

By and large, the American father has an attitude towards his children which may be loosely classified as autumnal. They are his for a brief and passing season, and in a very short while they will be operating gadgets which he does not understand and cockily talking a language to which he has no clue. He does his best to keep ahead of his son, takes a superior tone as long as he can, and knows that in nine cases out of ten he will lose. If the boy goes into his father's profession, of course, it will take him a time to catch up. He finds out that the old man knows a trick or two; that experience counts as over against this new-fangled nonsense. But the American boy solves that one very neatly: he typically does not go into his father's profession, nor take up land next to his father where his father can come over and criticize his plowing. He goes somewhere else, either in space or in occupation. And his father, who did the same thing and expects that his son will, is at heart terrifically disappointed if the son accedes to his ritual request that he docilely follow in his father's footsteps and secretly suspects the imitative son of being a milksop. He knows he is a milksop—or so he thinks—because he himself would have been a milksop if he had wanted to do just what his father did.

This passage was put before you as a source of new terms possibly applicable to the conflict you described in Theme 4 between yourself and your parents. What new terms? One obvious one is the phrase "mock battle," used by Margaret Mead to label certain "ceremonial" clashes between the generations in primitive societies. "Ceremony," "ritual," "primitive peoples"—these, of course, are basic English in the anthropologist's vocabulary. "Generation after generation the old men lose," she says (page 55). "The members of the tribe who are fighting the mock battle consciously or unconsciously know the outcome and fight with no less display of zeal for the knowing of it."

"So it is," she goes on, "in American society." At this point we remind ourselves that we are not trying to determine here whether Margaret Mead is "right" about this, whether is really *is* so in American society. That is a job beyond the limits of an English course. Our question is, Can the phrase "mock battle" be used to discuss your situation, or not? This is an attempt at a kind of translation, from one world of language to another.

Before trying to make your translation, we might properly ask whether it would be possible to apply Mead's anthropology-talk to Sinclair Lewis' novel-talk. Is the family conflict in *Babbitt* described by Lewis in such a way that it might be reseen from the point of view of—using the vocabulary of—the anthropologist?

To attempt this, you could make a list of some of the phrases

Margaret Mead uses as she applies her term "mock battle" to the American scene. Here are some obvious ones, in the same paragraph beginning, "So it is in American society":

> lack the sure hand on the rudder
> conventional and superficial grumbling
> neurotic father
> neurotic son or daughter
> ceremonial grumbling

Could any of these terms be used as ways of seeing the conflict between father and children in the Babbitt family? Easily. Babbitt is portrayed as lacking a "sure hand on the rudder" in the sense that his efforts to dictate to his children dissolve in impotent oratory. In the episode of the car, for instance, and Ted's intention to use it that night, Babbitt snorts, "May want it myself!" but later the children make their own efficient disposition of the car without consulting Father at all. Father's "grumbling" has surely been "superficial." There are no neurotics in this family, in Mead's sense, for no one takes the battle cries in the family war quite seriously. Even Babbitt's final statement on his family life, which seems so solemn and tragic, melts quickly away. "I simply can't stand it," he complains, but in the very same speech he loses the thread of his complaint and changes the subject. "Curious; here in the paper it says—"

On the other hand there are plenty of terms in Mead that simply are not relevant to the selection from *Babbitt*. Consider, for example, her term "ritual request," in the passage in which she argues that the American father "is at heart terrifically disappointed" if his son docilely follows in his father's profession. Perhaps this term might be made relevant to your own Theme 4, though it is not to *Babbitt*. If your conflict involved the issue of a career you planned to enter, does the term "ritual request" provide another, possibly even a useful, way of describing the incident? Or perhaps it does not; that is, you may decide that your parent's "request" to have you follow in his own footsteps was not "ritual" at all but thoroughly serious. In that case you would be arguing that the translation would be a bad one, and you should show your reasons for so believing.

DIRECTIONS FOR THEME 5

REWRITE—THAT IS, RESEE—YOUR FAMILY CONFLICT OF THEME 4 IN THE LIGHT OF SOME OF THE NEW TERMS YOU HAVE ENCOUNTERED IN THE LANGUAGE OF MARGARET MEAD. SHOW IN DETAIL HOW ONE OR MORE OF HER PHRASES MIGHT PROVIDE A TRANSLATION OF YOUR EXPERIENCE FROM ANOTHER POINT OF VIEW. IS THIS A USEFUL TRANSLATION? WHY OR WHY NOT? FINALLY, EXPLAIN WHAT HAPPENS TO YOUR ORIGINAL EXPERIENCE WHEN YOU TRANSLATE IT IN THIS MANNER. DOES THE EXPERIENCE CHANGE TOO?

6   SEEING SCHOOL DAYS

Treacherous though memory is, it seems to me the chief means we have of discovering how a child's mind works. Only by resurrecting our own memories can we realize how incredibly distorted is the child's vision of the world.

—GEORGE ORWELL

The next problem is the seeing of another autobiographical experience—this time a reminiscence of school days. The reading is taken from a book called *A Walker in the City,* in which the author revisits some scenes of his boyhood in that section of Brooklyn known as Brownsville. Here is the way the book begins:

Every time I go back to Brownsville it is as if I had never been away. From the moment I step off the train at Rockaway Avenue and smell the leak out of the men's room, then the pickles from the stand just below the subway steps, an instant rage comes over me, mixed with dread and some unexpected tenderness. It is over ten years since I left to live in "the city"—everything just out of Brownsville was always "the city." Actually I did not go very far; it was enough that I could leave Brownsville. Yet as I walk those

61

familiarly choked streets at dusk and see the old women sitting in front of the tenements, past and present become each other's faces; I am back where I began.

Whenever we read a piece of writing, we have an experience similar to listening to someone speak. In both cases, words are addressed to us, or to someone else, and we infer from the way the words are used the sort of person who is doing the speaking. Of course, when we are in a situation of being talked to by an actual person, we have many things to rely on in addition to words to increase our understanding, such as the way the speaker gestures, the way his voice rises and falls, the way he raises his eyebrows. In written language we have only words. As you examine the words that the "person speaking" is uttering in this paragraph, what can you tell about him—about the kind of person he is, about his attitudes and personality?

Actually you can tell a good deal, just from the way the language is chosen and arranged. For instance, would you say that this speaker talks like a product typical of this immigrant section of Brooklyn? Or is it rather that, in spite of the tawdriness of the scene he describes, he is in fact using a highly educated voice, a voice of the sort which, were we to encounter it in person, we would describe as intelligent and sensitive? Obviously the second is true, and you can find your evidence in the second sentence. Here the voice describes a decidedly unpretty or "tough" spectacle, and he minces no words, but his response is not a simple or crude affair. Immediately after the men's room and the pickles, which he "sees," like one of our blind men from Theme 2, a complex and well-considered statement of feeling follows: not just rage, but rage "mixed with dread" and "unexpected tenderness." That tenderness is unexpected by the reader too. It is as if the vulgarity of the scene were balanced by the sensibility of the speaker's own mind—perhaps as it has developed since leaving Brownsville. We can see another sort of balance between past and present in the way the paragraph begins and ends: ". . . it is as if I had never been away" and "I am back where I began." The same balance appears in a single clause "past and present become each other's faces." We are listening, in short, to a man who is in control of his voice.

A few pages later, this man, telling us of his return to his boyhood community after ten years' absence, begins to speak of his old school, and that is the subject that particularly concerns us here:

Brownsville School Days

by ALFRED KAZIN

All my early life lies open to my eye within five city blocks. When I passed the school, I went sick with all my old fear of it. With its standard New York public-school brown brick courtyard shut in on three sides of the square and the pretentious battlements overlooking that cockpit in which I can still smell the fiery sheen of the rubber ball, it looks like a factory over which has been imposed the façade of a castle. It gave me the shivers to stand up in that courtyard again; I felt as if I had been mustered back into the service of those Friday morning "tests" that were the terror of my childhood.

It was never learning I associated with that school: only the necessity to succeed, to get ahead of the others in the daily struggle to "make a good impression" on our teachers, who grimly, wearily, and often with ill-concealed distaste watched against our relapsing into the natural savagery they expected of Brownsville boys. The white, cool, thinly ruled record book sat over us from their desks all day long, and had remorselessly entered into it each day—in blue ink if we had passed, in red ink if we had not—our attendance, our conduct, our "effort," our merits and demerits; and to the last possible decimal point in calculation, our standing in an unending series of "tests"—surprise tests, daily tests, weekly tests, formal mid-term tests, final tests. They never stopped trying to dig out of us whatever small morsel of fact we had managed to get down the night before. We had to prove that we were really alert, ready for anything, always in the race. That white thinly ruled record book figured in my mind as the judgment seat; the very thinness and re-mote blue lightness of its lines instantly showed its cold authority over me; so much space had been left on each page, columns and columns in which to note down everything about us, implacably and forever. As it lay there on a teacher's desk, I stared at it all day long with such fear and anxious propriety that I had no trouble believing that God, too, did nothing but keep such record books, and that on the final day He would face me with an account in Hebrew letters whose phonetic dots and dashes looked strangely like decimal points counting up my every sinful thought on earth.

All teachers were to be respected like gods, and God Himself was the greatest of all school superintendents. Long after I had ceased to believe that our teachers could see with the back of their heads, it was still understood, by me, that they knew everything. They were the delegates of all visible and invisible power on earth—of the mothers who waited on the stoops every day after three for us to bring home tales of our daily triumphs; of the glacially remote Anglo-Saxon principal, whose very name was King; of the incal-culably important Superintendent of Schools who would someday rubberstamp his name to the bottom of our diplomas in grim acknowledgment that we had, at last, given satisfaction to him, to the Board of Superintendents, and to our benefactor the City of New York—and so up and up, to the government of the United States and to the great Lord Jehovah Himself. My belief in teach-ers' unlimited wisdom and power rested not so much on what I saw in them—how impatient most of them looked, how wary—but on our abysmal humility, at least in those of us who were "good" boys, who proved by our ready compliance and "manners" that we wanted to get on. The road to a professional future would be shown us only as we pleased *them*. *Make a good impression the first day of the term, and they'll help you out. Make a bad impression, and you might as well cut your throat.* This was the first article of school folklore, whispered around the classroom the opening day of each term. You made the "good impression" by sitting firmly at your wooden desk, hands clasped; by silence for the greatest part of the live-long day; by standing up obsequiously when it was so expected of you; by sitting down noiselessly when you had answered a question; by "speaking nicely," which meant reproducing their painfully exact enunciation; by "showing manners," or an ecstatic submissiveness in all things; by outrageous flattery; by bringing little gifts at Christmas, on their birthdays, and at the end of the term—the well-known significance of these gifts being that they came not from us, but from our parents, whose eagerness in this matter showed a high level of social consideration, and thus raised our standing in turn.

It was not just our quickness and memory that were always being tested. Above all, in that word I could never hear without automatically seeing it raised before me in gold-plated letters, it was our *character*. I always felt anxious when I heard the word pronounced. Satisfactory as my "character" was, on the whole, except when I stayed too long in the playground reading; outrageously satisfactory, as I can see now, the very sound of the word as our teachers coldly gave it out from the end of their teeth, with a solemn weight on each dark syllable, immediately struck my heart cold with fear— they could not believe I really had it. Character was never something you had; it had to be trained in you, like a technique. I was never very clear about it. On our side *character* meant demonstrative obedience; but teachers already had it—how else could they have become teachers? They had it; the aloof Anglo-Saxon principal whom we remotely saw only on ceremonial occasions in the assembly was positively encased in it; it glittered off his bald head in spokes of triumphant light; the President of the United States had the greatest conceivable amount of it. Character belonged to great adults. Yet we were constantly being driven onto it; it was the great threshold we had to cross. *Alfred Kazin, having shown proficiency in his course of studies and having displayed satisfactory*

marks of character . . . Thus someday the hallowed diploma, pass-
port to my further advancement in high school. But there—I could
already feel it in my bones—they would put me through even more
doubting tests of character; and after that, if I should be good
enough and bright enough, there would be still more. *Character* was
a bitter thing, racked with my endless striving to please. The school
—from every last stone in the courtyard to the battlements frowning
down at me from the walls—was only the stage for a trial. I felt that
the very atmosphere of learning that surrounded us was fake—that
every lesson, every book, every approving smile was only a pretext
for the constant probing and watching of me, that there was not a
secret in me that would not be decimally measured into that white
record book. All week long I lived for the blessed sound of the dis-
missal gong at three o'clock on Friday afternoon.

I was awed by this system, I believed in it, I respected its force.
The alternative was "going bad." The school was notoriously the
toughest in our tough neighborhood, and the dangers of "going
bad" were constantly impressed upon me at home and in school in
dark whispers of the "reform school" and in examples of boys who
had been picked up for petty thievery, rape, or flinging a heavy ink-
well straight into a teacher's face. Behind any failure in school
yawned the great abyss of a criminal career. Every refractory attitude doomed you with the sound "Sing Sing." Anything less than
absolute perfection in school always suggested to my mind that I
might fall out of the daily race, be kept back in the working class
forever, or—dared I think of it?—fall into the criminal class itself.

I worked on a hairline between triumph and catastrophe. Why
the odds should always have felt so narrow I understood only when
I realized how little my parents thought of their own lives. It was
not for myself alone that I was expected to shine, but for them—
to redeem the constant anxiety of their existence. I was the first
American child, their offering to the strange new God; I was to be
the monument of their liberation from the shame of being—what
they were. And that there was shame in this was a fact that everyone seemed to believe as a matter of course. It was in the gleeful

discounting of themselves—what do we know?—with which our parents greeted every fresh victory in our savage competition for "high averages," for prizes, for a few condescending words of official praise from the principal at assembly. It was in the sickening invocation of "Americanism"—the word itself accusing us of everything we apparently were not. Our families and teachers seemed tacitly agreed that we were somehow to be a little ashamed of what we were. Yet it was always hard to say why this should be so. It was certainly not—in Brownsville!—because we were Jews, or simply because we spoke another language at home, or were absent on our holy days. It was rather that a "refined," "correct," "nice" English was required of us at school that we did not naturally speak, and that our teachers could never be quite sure we would keep. This English was peculiarly the ladder of advancement. Every future young lawyer was known by it. Even the Communists and Socialists on Pitkin Avenue spoke it. It was bright and clean and polished. We were expected to show it off like a new pair of shoes. When the teacher sharply called a question out, then your name, you were expected to leap up, face the class, and eject those new words fluently off the tongue.

There was my secret ordeal: I could never say anything except in the most roundabout way; I was a stammerer. Although I knew all those new words from my private reading—I read walking in the street, to and from the Children's Library on Stone Avenue; on the fire escape and the roof; at every meal when they would let me; read even when I dressed in the morning, propping my book up against the drawers of the bureau as I pulled on my long black stockings—I could never seem to get the easiest words out with the right dispatch, and would often miserably signal from my desk that I did not know the answer rather than get up to stumble and fall and crash on every word. If, angry at always being put down as lazy or stupid, I did get up to speak, the black wooden floor would roll away under my feet, the teacher would frown at me in amazement, and in unbearable loneliness I would hear behind me the groans and laughter: *tuh-tuh-tuh-tuh*.

The word was my agony. The word that for others was so effortless and so neutral, so unburdened, so simple, so exact, I had first to meditate in advance, to see if I could make it, like a plumber fitting together odd lengths and shapes of pipe. I was always preparing words I could speak, storing them away, choosing between them. And often, when the word did come from my mouth in its great and terrible birth, quailing and bleeding as if forced through a thornbush, I would not be able to look the others in the face, and would walk out in the silence, the infinitely echoing silence behind my back, to say it all cleanly back to myself as I walked in the streets. Only when I was alone in the open air, pacing the roof with pebbles in my mouth, as I had read Demosthenes had done to cure himself of stammering; or in the street, where all words seemed to flow from the length of my stride and the color of the houses as I remembered the perfect tranquillity of a phrase in Beethoven's *Romance in F* I could sing back to myself as I walked—only then was it possible for me to speak without the infinite premeditations and strangled silences I toiled through whenever I got up at school to respond with the expected, the exact answer.

It troubled me that I could speak in the fullness of my own voice only when I was alone on the streets, walking about. There was something unnatural about it; unbearably isolated. I was not like the others! I was not like the others! At midday, every freshly shocking Monday noon, they sent me away to a speech clinic in a school in East New York, where I sat in a circle of lispers and cleft palates and foreign accents holding a mirror before my lips and rolling difficult sounds over and over. To be sent there in the full light of the opening week, when everyone else was at school or going about his business, made me feel as if I had been expelled from the great normal body of humanity. I would gobble down my lunch on my way to the speech clinic and rush back to the school in time to make up for the classes I had lost. One day, one unforgettable dread day, I stopped to catch my breath on a corner of Sutter Avenue, near the wholesale fruit markets, where an old drugstore rose up over a great flight of steps. In the window were dusty urns of colored water floating off iron chains; cardboard placards advertising hairnets, Ex-Lax; a great illustrated medical chart headed THE HUMAN

FACTORY, which showed the exact course a mouthful of food follows as it falls from chamber to chamber of the body. I hadn't meant to stop there at all, only to catch my breath; but I so hated the speech clinic that I thought I would delay my arrival for a few minutes by eating my lunch on the steps. When I took the sandwich out of my bag, two bitterly hard pieces of hard salami slipped out of my hand and fell through a grate onto a hill of dust below the steps. I remember how sickeningly vivid an odd thread of hair looked on the salami, as if my lunch were turning stiff with death. The factory whistles called their short, sharp blasts stark through the middle of noon, beating at me where I sat outside the city's magnetic circle. I had never known, I knew instantly I would never in my heart again submit to, such wild passive despair as I felt at that moment, sitting on the steps before THE HUMAN FACTORY, where little robots gathered and shoveled the food from chamber to chamber of the body. They had put me out into the streets, I thought to myself; with their mirrors and their everlasting pulling at me to imitate their effortless bright speech and their stupefaction that a boy could stammer and stumble on every other English word he carried in his head, they had put me out into the streets, had left me high and dry on the steps of that drugstore staring at the remains of my lunch turning black and grimy in the dust.

Now you are ready to write your own reminiscence of your own school days. Your memories are perhaps not so unhappy as Kazin's, and they are probably different from his in many other ways. But you have two problems, as a writer, that you share with him, and that you must consider carefully as you write.

The first is the matter of your own speaking voice, that person that you become as you address yourself to your reader. This is the same issue we mentioned in relation to Mark Twain's innocent mask in Theme 3, and the general question of how an "I" is to be dramatized. You may not want to adopt the kind of voice that Kazin uses, with that tough-and-tender vocabulary we mentioned in his opening paragraph. But you must more or less consciously choose *some* sort of voice, some speaking personality, to express what you have to say, and you must try to keep that voice consistent from sentence to sentence and paragraph to paragraph. You can write a funny reminiscence if you want, but, if you do, don't try to end with some solemn conclusion that changes your tone. If you decide you're going to speak in an informal, easy sort of way (as in this very sentence, with its contraction and use of the second person), do not abruptly alter your mode of address to a more pontifical guise (as in this part of this sentence). Obviously your teacher will expect from you, whatever your decision, a reasonably mature speaking voice worthy of a student in college.

The second problem you share with Kazin, and a serious one in every theme, is the problem of deciding just how much you can say within your limits of space. You won't be writing anywhere near as long an article as his, and you must certainly restrict the area of experience you choose accordingly. If you try to talk about your school days *in general,* then clearly your writing will be general, and probably dull. The most useful device for overcoming this difficulty is the one Kazin himself employs near the end of his reminiscence: he tells in detail about something that happened to him. Reread the story of the salami and The Human Factory to see how he does it. This is not simply an account of an incidental occurrence, of course. It has a meaning for him; he has made it stand for or signify a whole attitude toward his school days, his teachers, his loneliness. In some similar way, you would be wise to select a *particular incident* that once happened to you, and that you can use to stand for *your* remembrance of a certain time of your life. You will be *seeing* this incident, then, as meaningful for you.

DIRECTIONS FOR THEME 6

WRITE A DESCRIPTION OF YOUR OWN SCHOOL DAYS IN WHICH
YOU FOCUS ON A PARTICULAR INCIDENT, IN CLASS OR ELSE-
WHERE, THAT SEEMS TO YOU TO DRAMATIZE YOUR ATTITUDE
TOWARD YOUR SCHOOL AND YOUR TEACHERS AT A PARTICULAR
PERIOD OF YOUR LIFE.

7

SCHOOL DAYS AS PSYCHOLOGY

We wish to make the ego the object of our study, our own ego. But how can we do that? The ego is the subject par excellence, *how can it become the object? There is no doubt, however, that it can. The ego can take itself as object, it can treat itself like any other object, observe itself, criticize itself, and do Heaven knows what besides with itself.*

—FREUD

The next passage for reading is taken from a talk delivered to a group of prospective teachers by a psychologist and counselor of college students. The voice you will be hearing is a far different voice from the serious, sensitive one you heard in Kazin. This voice is easy, informal, colloquial—the voice of a *talker* speaking to a group of interested intelligent people on a difficult subject, but determined not to be too solemn about it. Most of his language accordingly is simple, as in conversation. "I am going to draw a kind of chart," he announces at the end of the first paragraph, and notice that it's not just a chart alone that he's going to draw, but "a kind of chart," reminding us of the modesty of his ambitions. He goes on: ". . . in the hope that it may keep us from becoming utterly lost." This suggests that we will become *somewhat* lost anyway, chart or no chart. It's very relaxing to know that not too much is expected of us.

Conflicts in the Learning Process

by WILLIAM G. PERRY, Jr.

What I am going to do is to try to explore how the educational world looks to the student—perhaps, indeed, how the world itself looks. By this I don't mean what he will or can tell you about it; I mean, rather, what his assumptions are and what his frame of reference is, the more or less unconscious basis of his behavior. Here I am launching those tentative suppositions in which one must explore the sea of one's ignorance. I am going to draw a kind of chart in the hope that it may keep us from becoming utterly lost.

When we as children first come into the world and look around to see what the world is made of, we see soon enough that the world is made of They. And what are They like? They tell us, do they not, what we *ought to* do? They tell us our *duty*. They tell us what is *necessary*. And it is necessary to do a lot of things that we don't like in the world, so They say. It is necessary to do a lot of things that are unpleasant. So that this business that They tell us about is by their own account *unpleasant*. So this is the world and its demands.

But now, as I look at this world, I begin to think of my own individuality and separateness, and I say to myself, "Who's Me?" Well, I am little and I am helpless, but I obviously have to be something quite different from all this if I am going to have any differentness, any individuality, which seems so precious to me. And what is the opposite to all that They stand for? Why, it is obviously what I *want.* So it follows that my individuality and my integrity, for which I will fight to the death, consists of what I want—that is, of my *wishes*—all of which I associate with the *pleasant:*

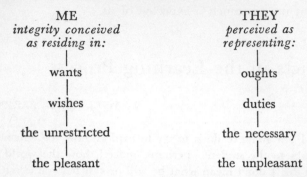

ME *integrity conceived as residing in:*	THEY *perceived as representing:*
wants	oughts
wishes	duties
the unrestricted	the necessary
the pleasant	the unpleasant

Clearly, now, I am faced at once with a number of serious difficulties. In the first place my integrity demands that I get what I want. If I do not, I am not only frustrated, I am much worse than that: I am somehow less Me. On the other hand, a lot of things that I want can be attained only through They, and They disapprove of other things that I want. If I do not give up these tabooed wants and do a certain amount of the unpleasant, then They will not love me any more, and that would be fatal to all my wishes. Furthermore, I may feel in part genuinely fond of They in that They do give me some things I want. Another difficulty is still more confusing. I soon discover, let us say at the age of three or four, or five, that They got me so young, when I was unable to defend myself, that They went and put a little bit of They in Me and I can't get away from it; it keeps nagging me all the time.

The dilemma is very serious indeed, and is made worse by the conflicting nature of my wishes. I wish to be dominant and independent; I wish also to be dependent and loved. However, I blind myself to this internal source of difficulty and concentrate on what seems the external problem of getting what I want and placating They. There are all sorts of attempted solutions to this almost insoluble problem. The most obvious one is the Social Contract of Rousseau—that is, the compromise. In this solution I simply do a number of the things that They say I ought to do, and then I hope that

They will leave me alone to go forth and do some of the things that I want. The trouble with this solution is that the compromise never really seems to be accepted by either side; both sides seem to be trying to beat the game and to ask for more. It is a very uneasy situation. I do some of the things that I want to do for a while; then I get a guilty conscience and do some of the things that I ought to do for a while; then I feel frustrated and so I go and do what I want to do, and then I get conscience-stricken again, and back and forth, back and forth, I go. And all this time the sensation keeps piling up that somebody is wasting time.

We might digress for a moment here and look at a curious application of this Social Contract in the educational world. It is perfectly clear to Me, in the educational world, that what They want is for me to be good; what They want is for me to do my duty, which is to sit down and do this studying that I have been given to do. If I do that, their part of the bargain is that They will give me the good grade that I want, so we get the curious formula which you find running throughout education, namely: work through time equals grades. This is a kind of basic moral law. It does not matter what I say on an examination; if I have done the work I should get the grade, and if my roommate, who has done none of the work, reads my notes before the examination and goes in and gets a higher grade than I do, that shows that They are unfair.

We might digress a little further. My integrity, my sense of Meness is bound up with my wishes, and since They invade my integrity with all these "don'ts" and "ought's," and since the Social Contract is not working very well and I am getting a little resentful, it is very natural for me to decide that I really could have everything that I wanted if it were not for They; given half a chance I would prove as omnipotent as I secretly believe myself to be. This feeling, which we have all shared, is exemplified by a student who once said: "I really could cut loose from everything; I could cut loose from my parents and my wife and from everything, just as a friend of mine has done who is now down in Ceylon. I could do that, only I don't think I ought to. I could be really perfectly independent and get everything that I wanted. I just don't do it because I don't think I *should*. Besides that, of course, I gain such satisfactions from my

family." I said, "You mean that if you went to Ceylon you wouldn't
have those satisfactions that you want?" He replied, "No." He was
still blind to his contradiction. Then suddenly it struck him, and he
said, "This is the first time I've ever realized that I couldn't really
have everything I wanted if it wasn't for them."

If it is natural and easy for us to engage in this kind of thinking
about our omnipotence, we can carry it one step further. I shall
bethink me of the future; I shall conjure up an ideal picture of what
I shall become. I shall be a doctor, a really great doctor; I shall be
so clever that everyone will admire me, and I shall know so much
that I can do anything I want. Now it is a highly commendable
thing to be a good doctor and to make discoveries that will ease
the lot of the human race, and here, you see, is where I satisfy They,
especially the They of my own conscience. So here I have an ideal
which seems to satisfy both my need for independence or power
and my conscience. There is only one trouble with it—the minute
that I try to put it into action, They get in my way again; They
require that I study German and various aspects of physics and literature which will be really of no use to me. Naturally, it is an invasion
of my integrity to study these requirements and somehow I have
a terrible time with them. "I won't eat those beans if They tell me
to; no matter how good they may be, no matter how fine the dessert,
it is not worth the price of my integrity, and I won't do it." Or if
my revolt is not as conscious as this, I will simply relegate doing
them until "tomorrow."

We had better not digress any more, for we could probably digress
forever and still have an over-simple picture of the matter. It is
my opinion, anyway, that from the particular point of view of
which we have been speaking—that is, the child's point of view—
the problems of life are actually insoluble. It has always been my
suspicion that Rousseau never quite grew up. Let us go back to the
point where we felt that in the midst of all these attempted solutions
somebody was wasting time.

It is this very notion of time that is crucial. Until now we have
made no mention of time. Time is an aspect of reality, and we have
made no mention whatever of reality. To the child there is no such
thing as reality directly; there is only what They say is necessary,

and even when what They say is necessary or real actually happens, even that appears to be just an "I-told-you-so" of grown-ups. Time, as one aspect of reality, does not apply to Me. In fact Me is at its most omnipotent in the timelessness of tomorrow. One of the most obvious solutions to the dilemma of the Me is to do what I want to do today and do what I ought to do tomorrow. Perhaps it is in large part through this sensation of wasting time that reality first comes into awareness—that I get my first glimpse of just plain fact. It is this stunning revelation of the factual, the notion that I cannot go to Ceylon and have everything that I want, that breaks down utterly the dichotomy of the They and the Me. And here we are on the brink of maturity. For now that this dichotomy is broken down, we can have a look at the frame of reference from which the sensation that I have been wasting time arises. The whole sensation implies a new value system, some wholly different frame of reference in which defending the integrity of my wishes is not what I really want to be doing. Here it is that I discover that the person who has been wasting time is my Self.

It is upon the difference between the Me and the Self that everything that I have to say hinges. The difference is one of essential personal identity; it is a felt difference that concerns who I am—that concerns what makes up, for me, my personal individuality. We have already seen that for the child identity is conceived as consisting of wishes, especially those wishes which the child holds in contradistinction of They. No internal conflict or contradiction is accepted among these wishes; all conflict is projected and seems to be externally imposed. But for the Self wishes suddenly lose their distinctive and individual character. I suddenly perceive that everyone has much the same wishes, and furthermore I see these wishes as an aspect of fact and reality. They then lose their glorious simplicity and can be seen in all the conflict and complexity which is really theirs. For the first time, therefore, I am confronted with the real issue of *choice*. The individuality and integrity of the Self is therefore conceived to reside not in my wishes, but in the act of choosing in the midst of the complexity of reality. This reality consists not only of my wishes, but also of society and of physical limitations, including that of time. Up until now I had confused freedom with independence; now I realize that freedom is not the independence to follow one's wishes, but the act of choice among personal values. And personal values for my Self include not only wishes in the narrow sense of impulses, but also objective purposes in a real world *and* many of those responsibilities and obligations and duties which I have previously seen only as the demands of They. In this new frame of reference it is no longer either a loss of integrity, or an act of masochism, to do something unpleasant; it may be simply useful or productive. And though I still have both my wishes and my "ought's," my integrity is not at issue between them; it is, in fact, expressed in my act of choice whichever way I choose in relation to a particular set of circumstances in reality.

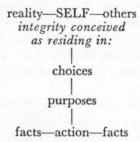

reality—SELF—others
integrity conceived
as residing in:
|
choices
|
purposes
|
facts—action—facts

As an illustration we might consider the matter of the language requirement. Almost all colleges and graduate schools have a language requirement, and as students we buck it. It is a great symbol, the language requirement; it is the last great apotheosis of Their incredible and unreasonable demands. When it comes time to sit down and do that German, we read the newspaper, we read *Life,* we sharpen our pencils, we do anything to delay the awful moment. When finally we do get to work, we do just what we feel we are "required" to do: we turn the word-cards over, we translate word by word from this or that, and if nothing comes from all our labors, it is not our fault, it is Theirs; and the fact that nothing ever seems to come out of it just goes to show how right we are. The language requirement appears as a price we are forced to pay for a degree which They withhold. It obviously is not the business of a Me, it is just a requirement of They, and I spend a great deal of time expanding upon its archaism and injustice. From the point of view of the Self, however, the matter looks very different indeed. You have come to this store of your own choice, to buy a certain article, an A.B. or a Ph.D. And how in this store does this article come packaged; in what form does it appear on the counter? It always includes the language requirement. It is not, if you please, a price that you pay, but rather part of the product that you buy. You may not want this accessory, you understand, you may not consider it reasonable, and you may wish that the product came packaged without it; but if the management is not disposed to change the package, you have, in fact, a choice of taking the article or leaving it. If you choose to take it, it is not an invasion of your integrity to fulfill the language requirement; it is, in fact, an expression of your own choice in regard to reality; and because the Self is primarily the chooser, it is an act of Self-expression. Certainly it may be unpleasant or dull, and even frustrating of other purposes that you would like to substitute for it; but for the Self, frustration is not purely an imposition from the outside and a threat to integrity; rather it is one of the conditions of life, because even my own wishes are often incompatible. Hence, dull or not, it can be done with a will.

In the event that you have been subscribing at all to this, you have probably been looking at yourself, if not with alarm, at least with some concern, with the question, "Am I a Me or am I a Self? Am I a child or am I an adult?" I doubt that you will find a ready answer. The question would have been prompted by the way I have been presenting this. I have seemed to imply that a person is either a child or an adult, but this is because such things as authority, necessity, and the unpleasant are so sharply different in quality when looked at from the two points of view that there are really no in-betweens; it is an all-or-none proposition. The two frames of reference are separate, distinct, and self-contained, but what makes growth into maturity look like a gradual thing is, I think, first that we take the point of view of Self in one area of life at a time and, second, that even in those areas in which we have attained it, it is notoriously unstable. A student, for instance, may attain a mature frame of reference in his social relationships and remain a child in his school work. He may feel and act as an adult in his summer job and in the fall drag his feet, as a pupil, reluctantly to school. He

may feel and act as an adult away from home, but when he returns
to the famly that treats him as a child, he will feel like one. It is this
jumping back and forth from one frame of reference to another that
is the basis, I believe, of the instability of adolescence. Of course it
stays with us, to a degree, all our lives.

So far I have painted the frame of reference of the Self as so
much more comfortable and desirable that this critical instability
may seem strange. Let us have a look at a few of its discomforts.
Being a Self is a very risky and frightening business. As a Me I still
have claims on that day when things go wrong in life. When I fail,
when I am disappointed, when I am hurt, I can call on Them for
comfort, for love, for reassurance, for protection. If I am a Self, I
no longer have these claims in anything like the same degree. In fact
I am alone, and I have not yet learned that to be alone, as all
human beings are, is not necessarily to be lonely. Hardest of all, I
must, to be a Self, allow my wishes, my omnipotence, and my fan-
tasies to suffer real defeats in the face of reality. I may never be a
really great doctor, and to be even a mediocre one, or even a failure,
I must sweat. Even if I turn out to have ability and have worked
hard, just plain circumstances may defeat me. Can I stand this without the compensation of Their sympathy and support, without being
able to demand that They play fair? And deeper down than any of
this, can I really trust my Self? If I try to rely on choice instead of
upon the compulsions of "ought's" and "must's," will I ever get
anything done?

We might take this last question and see how the fear operates to
tip us out of the mature frame of reference. Suppose that I am approaching my academic work, and the language requirement too,
with all kinds of maturity. I have kept in mind my own choice; I
have come to this institution because I chose to; I accept the language requirement as an aspect of reality; I accept the notion that
time applies to me; and I choose, therefore, to do the language requirement now rather than tomorrow. I am doing my German, and
my roommate comes in and asks me to make a fourth at bridge.
Now I enjoy bridge; furthermore I haven't played for quite some
time; furthermore I have been working very hard. I deserve (what
frame of reference does that word come from?) a bit of change, a

little relaxation. I am sorely tempted. Suddenly I am afraid. I am afraid that I will go and play bridge and not get that language requirement done. I suddenly lose confidence in the Self to choose wisely. I cannot say to my roommate or to myself, "That sounds nice, but I want to get this German done." I cannot voice a simple preference. Instead, I say, "No, I really *ought* to do my German, I really *must* get it done." Now understand me, it looks as if I have not capitulated. I have not said to myself that I can do the German "tomorrow" and I have not gone off to play bridge. But I have capitulated. I have lost confidence in my own capacity to choose, and I have called upon the "ought's" and the "should's" and the "must's" to compel me, to do the deciding for me; and in the next hour, how I will resent it! I have set They up again as my masters, and how I will buck them! I will feel frustrated, I will think about the bridge, and somehow I will defeat my efforts to learn anything. Of course I may be able to get something done for a while by glorying in a kind of masochistic righteousness, but I won't keep it up for long. My spell of self-righteousness will only give me the excuse for taking the whole week end off. From the mature point of view it would have been better had my Self actually chosen tó play bridge and to deal with the consequences. I am not arguing against the value of a conscience; I am saying that if we set up the conscience as our compulsive authority instead of as our guide, then we may react as children toward it. To rely entirely upon its compulsion is to surrender the integrity of the Self, to abnegate the function of choice. Until one has had a little experience with the Self, it is hard to believe that we, as people, could really *prefer* to do our work. We say, "I have to drive myself to work." Who is driving whom here? Self-expression is the act of doing what we as *whole* people prefer.

Perhaps we can turn now to the subject of education. I was talking with a student the other day who relied so heavily upon his conscience and upon his parents that though he had the intentions of doing college work, he could not see them as his own. Whenever he told himself that he ought to get to work, he sounded to himself so much like his parents that he resisted his own statements. There was a constant strife between the parent in him, who was trying to make him do things, and the child in him, who was in revolt. Things had gotten a little pressing just before examinations, and he had begun to do a little work. He had decided, he said, that the only trouble with him was that he had no incentive. "But recently," he said, "I've had a lot of incentive; in fact I can't remember being so incensed in all my life."

What I am trying to say is that being incensed may be the normal and appropriate state of mind of the young while being educated. Education is the way that we get at them. We force the culture upon them, the "do's" and the "don'ts" and the "ought's" and the "must's," and when they start doing these, can they eagerly espouse them and keep their integrity, or must they resist to live? Watch them. They go on slow-down strikes and become slow readers. They bewilder themselves by their "laziness." They appeal to you, in con-science-stricken despair. And when they do their work, is their main purpose to learn something or to placate you? It is very profitable and enlightening to look at the act of studying as the process of pla-cating authority in the educational world.

Does this sound extreme? I remember when I first went into the business of helping students to study better, more efficiently and all that. I assumed, of course, that everybody wants to be efficient—that is, to get the same results with the least effort—and for all I know this still may be a perfectly reasonable assumption. When a student came to me, I would try to show him how to be efficient. He would say, "Here are my notes. I take lots of notes. I don't really know what is the matter, I'm not getting anywhere, that's all. I've been working and working and working, but I don't get the grades." Well, he would have plenty of notes, all right, stacks of them, all very neatly arranged, and most of them copied right out of the book; so I would show him, as kindly as possible, how inefficient all this was, how he had written and written but hadn't learned a thing. And I would show him how to learn much more and to do about one-fourth of all that copy work, and then he would say, "I don't know why I didn't think of that before; why that's marvelous! Thank you so much, sir." And he would run off. In a few weeks I'd see him again and say, "How are you getting on these days?" And there would be that same mass of verbatim notes. And while I sat there, feeling that wave of the teacher's despair, the student would say,

"I tried your method, sir, really I did [whose method?], but I don't know, really, sir, it just seems *better* this way."

Now the student was right. I had been trying to give him an efficient way of learning something, whereas he already had a very efficient way of satisfying his conscience, which was what he was mainly trying to do. You cannot imagine a more efficient way to satisfy your conscience than sitting for hours and writing out those notes. The note goes from the book up one finger and one arm, and across the shoulders, and down the other arm onto the paper, and your mind and heart and soul can be off on something else more pleasant. No extra effort at all. Such a method for such a student is admirably designed to fit his purposes. Do you suppose, as a teacher, that your main problem will be your students' stupidity? Or does it begin to seem as if your main problem might be the extraordinary wisdom of their resistance? . . .

We have pointed out that the tone of voice in this article is easy, informal, conversational. We could examine the second paragraph as an example, and conclude that here the vocabulary and sentence structure are even childlike. Short words, little questions with little answers. But already, in that second paragraph, disguised behind the childish repetitions, a sort of "key term" appears, a piece of vocabulary that looks childish and vague but is in fact used in an almost technical sense. This is, of course, the term "They," carefully capitalized, to point as a child might point to parents, teachers, and adults generally in all their awful authority.

In the next paragraph comes a corollary key term: Me. These two words, together with "integrity" and a good many others that follow, make up a vocabulary no less professional and technical in its way than the "mock battle" and "ceremonial grumbling" of Margaret Mead.

You anticipate the problem of this theme. Here is a writer (or talker) who is describing the relation of the young to their elders, particularly to their schoolteachers, and he is using a particular set of terms to do it. Does any of what he is saying offer a fresh way of seeing yourself as a schoolboy or girl? Can you find, in the language of this easy-talking psychologist, some terms that could be applied to your situation as you described it in Theme 6?

As you reread this speech, then, make a list of some of these key terms that Perry uses in his own special sense, like Me-They and "integrity." When you have finished, you should be in a position to resee your school days.

DIRECTIONS FOR THEME 7

REWRITE YOUR SCHOOL DAYS BY RESEEING YOUR INCIDENT OF THEME 6, USING SOME OF PERRY'S KEY TERMS. WHAT HAPPENS TO YOUR SCHOOL DAYS WHEN YOU CHANGE YOUR TERMS IN THIS WAY? DO YOUR SCHOOL DAYS CHANGE TOO?

8

SEEING A CHURCH FAÇADE

> *The truth must be*
> *That you do not see, you experience, you feel,*
> *That the buxom eye brings merely its element*
> *To the total thing, a shapeless giant forced*
> *Upward.*
> > *Green were the curls upon that head.*
> > —WALLACE STEVENS

With Theme 8 we return to a problem of immediate visual seeing. How do you see a building? How do you see (for instance) the front of a church? Here we face some familiar difficulties which by now you ought to be able to approach with some confidence. What about point of view? All senses of this phrase are important. To describe the front of a church you will need a particular physical *point* to begin with, from which your steps or your moving eyes can carry your reader to various aspects of the church façade. These movements must, of course, be orderly. For example, one might begin with a general impression, as from a distance; then, approaching closer, one might let one's eyes

From "Poem Written at Morning" from *The Collected Poems of Wallace Stevens* by permission of the publisher, Alfred A. Knopf, Inc. Copyright 1942, 1954 by Wallace Stevens.

travel from bottom to top, or from top to bottom. In any case the reader must have an impression that he is being led to see this building in a fashion that has some connection with an actual experience of looking. But point of view in its other senses of attitude and tone of voice are, of course, important here too. Who are you, who should you be, as you speak to a reader about the appearance of a church?

The reading matter this time is inspirational—that is, the author is a man who elegantly handles all these problems, for your edification and delight. He is the great novelist Henry James, and he is taking us to a great church, the Cathedral of Notre-Dame at Chartres, a short distance from Paris. As you will see, he is in no hurry.

Chartres

by HENRY JAMES

The spring, in Paris, since it has fairly begun, has been enchanting. The sun and the moon have been blazing in emulation, and the difference between the blue sky of day and of night has been as slight as possible. There are no clouds in the sky, but there are little thin green clouds, little puffs of raw, tender verdure, entangled among the branches of the trees. All the world is in the street; the chairs and tables which have stood empty all winter before the doors of the cafés are at a premium; the theatres have become intolerably close; the puppet-shows in the Champs Élysées are the only form

From *Portraits of Places* (Boston: James R. Osgood & Co., 1884), copyright 1883 by James R. Osgood & Co. This essay was revised by James from a travel-letter he published originally in the New York *Tribune* in April, 1876. The original version has been reprinted elsewhere, in Henry James's *Parisian Sketches,* eds. Leon Edel and Ilse Dusoir Lind (New York: New York University Press, 1957).

of dramatic entertainment which seems consistent with the season. By way of doing honour, at a small cost, to this ethereal mildness, I went out the other day to the ancient town of Chartres, where I spent several hours, which I cannot consent to pass over as if nothing had happened. It is the experience of the writer of these lines, who likes nothing so much as moving about to see the world, that if one has been for a longer time than usual resident and stationary, there is a kind of overgrown entertainment in taking the train, even for a suburban goal; and that if one takes it on a charming April day, when there is a sense, almost an odour, of change in the air, the innocent pleasure is as nearly as possible complete. My accessibility to emotions of this kind amounts to an infirmity, and the effect of it was to send me down to Chartres in a shamelessly optimistic state of mind. I was so prepared to be entertained and pleased with everything that it is only a mercy that the cathedral happens really to be a fine building. If it had not been, I should still have admired it inordinately, at the risk of falling into heaven knows what aesthetic heresy. But I am almost ashamed to say how soon my entertainment began. It began, I think, with my hailing a little open carriage on the boulevard and causing myself to be driven to the Gare de l'Ouest—far away across the river, up the Rue Bonaparte, of art-student memories, and along the big, straight Rue de Rennes to the Boulevard Montparnasse. Of course, at this rate, by the time I reached Chartres—the journey is of a couple of hours—I had almost drained the cup of pleasure. But it was replenished at the station, at the buffet, from the pungent bottle of wine I drank with my breakfast. Here, by the way, is another excellent excuse for being delighted with any day's excursion in France —that wherever you are, you may breakfast to your taste. There may, indeed, if the station is very small, be no buffet; but if there is a buffet, you may be sure that civilisation—in the persons of a sympathetic young woman in a well-made black dress, and a rapid zealous, grateful waiter—presides at it. It was quite the least, as the French say, that after my breakfast I should have thought the cathedral, as I saw it from the top of the steep hill on which the town stands, rising high above the clustered houses, and seeming to

make of their red-roofed agglomeration a mere pedestal for its immense beauty, promised remarkably well. You see it so as you emerge
from the station, and then, as you climb slowly into town, you lose
sight of it. You perceive empty open *places,* and crooked shady
streets, in which two or three times you lose your way, until at last,
after more than once catching a glimpse, high above some slit between the houses, of the clear gray towers shining against the blue
sky, you push forward again, risk another short cut, turn another
interposing corner, and stand before the goal of your pilgrimage.

I spent a long time looking at this monument. I revolved around
it, like a moth around a candle; I went away and I came back; I
chose twenty different standpoints; I observed it during the different
hours of the day, and saw it in the moonlight as well as the sunshine.
I gained, in a word, a certain sense of familiarity with it; and yet I
despair of giving any coherent account of it. Like most French cathedrals, it rises straight out of the street, and is destitute of that setting
of turf and trees and deaneries and canonries which contribute so
largely to the impressiveness of the great English churches. Thirty
years ago a row of old houses was glued to its base and made their
back walls of its sculptured sides. These have been plucked away,
and, relatively speaking, the church is fairly isolated. But the little
square that surrounds it is deplorably narrow, and you flatten your
back against the opposite houses in the vain attempt to stand off
and survey the towers. The proper way to look at them would be
to go up in a balloon and hang poised, face to face with them, in
the blue air. There is, however, perhaps an advantage in being
forced to stand so directly under them, for this position gives you an
overwhelming impression of their height. I have seen, I suppose,
churches as beautiful as this one, but I do not remember ever to
have been so fascinated by superpositions and vertical effects. The
endless upward reach of the great west front, the clear, silvery tone
of its surface, the way three or four magnificent features are made
to occupy its serene expanse, its simplicity, majesty, and dignity—
these things crowd upon one's sense with a force that makes the act
of vision seem for the moment almost all of life. The impressions
produced by architecture lend themselves as little to interpretation

by another medium as those produced by music. Certainly there is
an inexpressible harmony in the façade of Chartres.

The doors are rather low, as those of the English cathedrals are
apt to be, but (standing three together) are set in a deep framework
of sculpture—rows of arching grooves, filled with admirable little
images, standing with their heels on each other's heads. The church,
as it now exists, except the northern tower, dates from the middle
of the thirteenth century, and these closely packed figures are full
of the grotesqueness of the period. Above the triple portals is a
vast round-topped window, in three divisions, of the grandest dimensions and the stateliest effect. Above this window is a circular aper-
ture, of huge circumference, with a double row of sculptured spokes
radiating from its centre and looking on its lofty field of stone as
expansive and symbolic as if it were the wheel of Time itself. Higher
still is a little gallery with a delicate balustrade, supported on a
beautiful cornice and stretching across the front from tower to
tower; and above this is a range of niched statues of kings—fifteen,
I believe, in number. Above the statues is a gable, with an image of
the Virgin and Child on its front, and another of Christ on its apex.
In the relation of all these parts there is such a high felicity that
while on the one side the eye rests on a great many large blanks
there is no approach on the other to poverty. The little gallery that
I have spoken of, beneath the statues of the kings, had for me a
peculiar charm. Useless, at its tremendous altitude, for other purposes, it seemed intended for the little images to step down and walk
about upon. When the great façade begins to glow in the late
afternoon light, you can imagine them strolling up and down their
long balcony in couples, pausing with their elbows on the balustrade,
resting their stony chins in their hands, and looking out, with their
little blank eyes, on the great view of the old French monarchy
they once ruled, and which now has passed away. The two great
towers of the cathedral are among the noblest of their kind. They
rise in solid simplicity to a height as great as the eye often troubles
itself to travel, and then suddenly they begin to execute a magnificent series of feats in architectural gymnastics. This is especially
true of the northern spire, which is a late creation, dating from the

sixteenth century. The other is relatively quiet; but its companion is a sort of tapering bouquet of sculptured stone. Statues and buttresses, gargoyles, arabesques and crockets pile themselves in successive stages, until the eye loses the sense of everything but a sort of architectural lacework. The pride of Chartres, after its front, is the two portals of its transepts—great dusky porches, in three divisions, covered with more images than I have time to talk about. Wherever you look, along the sides of the church, a time-worn image is niched or perched. The face of each flying buttress is garnished with one, with the features quite melted away.

The inside of the cathedral corresponds in vastness and grandeur to the outside—it is the perfection of gothic in its prime. But I looked at it rapidly, the place was so intolerably cold. It seemed to answer one's query of what becomes of the winter when the spring chases it away. The winter hereabouts has sought an asylum in Chartres cathedral, where it has found plenty of room and may reside in a state of excellent preservation until it can safely venture abroad again. I supposed I had been in cold churches before, but the delusion had been an injustice to the temperature of Chartres. The nave was full of the little padded chairs of the local bourgeoisie, whose faith, I hope for their comfort, is of good old red-hot complexion. In a higher temperature I should have done more justice to the magnificent old glass of the windows—which glowed through the icy dusk like the purple and orange of a winter sunset—and to the immense sculptured external casing of the choir. This latter is an extraordinary piece of work. It is a high gothic screen, shutting in the choir, and covered with elaborate bas-reliefs of the sixteenth and seventeenth centuries, representing scenes from the life of Christ and of the Virgin. Some of the figures are admirable, and the effect of the whole great semicircular wall, chiselled like a silver bowl, is superb. There is also a crypt of high antiquity, and, I believe, great interest, to be seen; but my teeth chattered a respectful negative to the sacristan who offered to guide me to it. It was so agreeable to stand in the warm outer air again, that I spent the rest of the day in it.

Although, besides its cathedral, Chartres has no very rare archi-

tectural treasures, the place is pictorial, in a shabby, third-rate, pov-
erty-stricken degree, and my observations were not unremunerative.
There is a little church of Saint-Aignan, of the sixteenth century,
with an elegant, decayed façade, and a small tower beside it, lower
than its own roof, to which it is joined, in unequal twinship, by a
single long buttress. Standing there with its crumbling Renaissance
doorway, in a kind of grass-grown alcove, it reminded me of certain
monuments that the tourist encounters in small Italian towns. Most
of the streets of Chartres are crooked lanes, winding over the face
of the steep hill, the summit of the hill being occupied by half a
dozen little open squares, which seem like reservoirs of the dulness
and stillness that flow through the place. In the midst of one of
them rises an old dirty brick obelisk, commemorating the glories of
the young General Marceau, of the first Republic—"Soldier at 16,
general at 23, he died at 27." Such memorials, when one comes upon
them unexpectedly, produce in the mind a series of circular waves
of feeling, like a splash in a quiet pond. Chartres gives us an impression of extreme antiquity, but it is an antiquity that has gone
down in the world. I saw very few of those stately little hôtels, with
pilastered fronts, which look so well in the silent streets of provin-
cial towns. The houses are mostly low, small, and of sordid aspect,
and though many of them have overhanging upper stories, and
steep, battered gables, they are rather wanting in character. I was
struck, as an American always is in small French and English towns,
with the immense number of shops, and their brilliant appearance,
which seems so out of proportion to any visible body of consumers.
At Chartres the shopkeepers must all feed upon each other, for,
whoever buys, the whole population sells. This population appeared
to consist mainly of several hundred brown old peasant women, in
the seventies and eighties, with their faces cross-hatched with wrinkles and their quaint white coifs drawn tightly over their weather-
blasted eye-brows. Labour-stricken grandams, all the world over,
are the opposite of lovely, for the toil that wrestles for its daily
bread, morsel by morsel, is not beautifying; but I thought I had
never seen the possibilities of female ugliness so variously embodied
as in the crones of Chartres. Some of them were leading small chil-

dren by the hand—little red-cheeked girls, in the close black caps
and black pinafores of humble French infancy—a costume which
makes French children always look like orphans. Others were guiding along the flinty lanes the steps of small donkeys, some of them
fastened into little carts, some with well-laden backs. These were
the only quadrupeds I perceived at Chartres. Neither horse nor
carriage did I behold, save at the station the omnibuses of the rival
inns—the "Grand Monarque" and the "Duc de Chartres"—which
glare at each other across the Grande Place. A friend of mine told me
that a few years ago, passing through Chartres, he went by night
to call upon a gentleman who lived there. During his visit it came
on to rain violently, and when the hour for his departure arrived
the rain had made the streets impassable. There was no vehicle to
be had, and my friend was resigning himself to a soaking. "You can
be taken of course in the sedan-chair," said his host with dignity.
The sedan-chair was produced, a couple of serving-men grasped
the handles, my friend stepped into it, and went swinging back—
through the last century—to the "Grand Monarque." This little
anecdote, I imagine, still paints Chartres socially.

Before dinner I took a walk on the planted promenade which
encircles the town—the Tour-de-ville it is called—much of which
is extremely picturesque. Chartres has lost her walls as a whole, but
here and there they survive, and play a desultory part in holding
the town together. In one place the rampart is really magnificent—
smooth, strong and lofty, curtained with ivy, and supporting on its
summit an old convent and its garden. Only one of the city-gates
remains—a narrow arch of the fourteenth century, flanked by two
admirable round towers, and preceded by a fosse. If you stoop a
little, as you stand outside, the arch of this hoary old gate makes a
capital setting for the picture of the interior of the town, and, on
the inner hill-top, against the sky, the large gray mass of the Cathedral. The ditch is full, and to right and to the left it flows along the
base of the mouldering wall, through which the shabby backs of
houses extrude, and which is garnished with little wooden galleries,
lavatories of the town's soiled linen. These little galleries are filled
with washerwomen, who crane over and dip their many-coloured

rags into the yellow stream. The old patched and interrupted wall, the ditch with its weedy edges, the spots of color, the white-capped laundresses in their little wooden cages—one lingers to look at it all.

The two paragraphs in which James actually encounters the façade of Chartres and tries to come to terms with it begin on page (88), and we might pause over this encounter to admire the way he does it.

The *point* from which James attempts to *view* the façade is complicated, and indeed its complication is in part his subject. He is playful, as well as eager and enthusiastic, as he approaches his point, in a physical sense, by walking through the crooked streets of Chartres, and his use of the second person forces a kind of sharing on the part of the reader. "You push forward again, risk another short cut, turn another interposing corner, and stand before the goal of your pilgrimage."

So here we are at last: the monument. Now James engages in a series of half-ludicrous backings and fillings, trying quite self-consciously to find a point of view where he can settle. "I revolved around it, like a moth around a candle; I went away and I came back; I chose twenty different standpoints." But the scene is too much. "I despair of giving any coherent account of it." (Does he really despair? What does he, what does he not, despair of?) Part of his problem of finding a place to stand, as he says in the next few sentences, is due to the general structure of the square, where "you flatten your back against the opposite houses in the vain attempt to stand off and survey the towers." Maybe a balloon would do it! But a truer cause of these difficulties is to be found in the inexpressible quality of the façade itself, as James indicates in the remainder of the paragraph: "endless upward reach," "clear, silvery tone," "simplicity, majesty, dignity." These abstractions imply by their very vagueness the difficulties the speaker is suffering in communication. Physically he has not been able to find a place to stand, but in any case, as a man working with words, he finds himself confronting a "vision" that is simply not translatable into language. The subject of this paragraph might be defined as the problem of finding a point of view and translating experience into words, and that problem ought to sound familiar to the student of these exercises. "There is an inexpressible harmony in the façade of Chartres." There is something inexpressible in *any* harmony.

But now to business, and the next paragraph beginning, "The doors are rather low." Granting all these difficulties, James seems to say, let us in our pedestrian way do what we can to describe what we see in the Chartres façade. (You should follow his progress on the photograph, as well as in the paragraph itself.) He begins with the doors, then, and his general route is upward: framework of sculpture around and above the doors, the "vast, round-topped window" above that, the rose window, the balustrade, the statues of kings, and the gable on top. After a flight of fancy about the kings strolling on the balcony, he proceeds upward to the towers, where words again begin to fail. The "architectural gymnastics" of the north tower can be described only in lists of nouns like gargoyles and arabesques, "until the eye loses the sense of everything but a sort of architectural lacework." And he changes the subject, to the transepts.

An important function of this style is its repeated reminder that no style can adequately control such experience. The speaker protests his incapacity throughout, and finally, like any tourist, he turns away with some relief to the shabby town, the touching obelisk, and his dinner.

The problem for you, the student writer, is of course not to sound like Henry James (which has been tried), but to see your own church with your own sensibility and your own style.

DIRECTIONS FOR THEME 8

FIND A CHURCH IN YOUR NEIGHBORHOOD THAT SEEMS TO YOU AN INTERESTING BUILDING. DESCRIBE WHAT YOU SEE ON ITS FAÇADE IN DETAIL, AND IN SUCH A STYLE THAT YOUR READER SEES IT AS AN INTERESTING BUILDING TOO.

9

THE FAÇADE AS HISTORY

Nothing in education is so astonishing as the amount of ignorance it accumulates in the form of inert facts.

—HENRY ADAMS

There are plenty of other points of view from which one might see a church façade. There are other terms available, in addition to those of the modestly elegant observer whose language we admired in Theme 8. An engineer could see the façade in terms of stresses and construction materials; an atheist could call it pablum for the masses; an artist could admire that "glow in the late afternoon light" and reach for his chrome yellow. This list could be protracted. The terms you are about to encounter, however, are those of a historian. The problem in this theme is to determine, so far as one sparkling example can help, how a historian uses his particular language to talk about the façade of Chartres Cathedral, and how you might do likewise with your own church.

You might want to point out that there are some places in the essay by Henry James (who was no historian) where historical statements are made. For instance, James calls the northern tower "a late creation, dating from the sixteenth century." Isn't this as historical a remark as one could want? Maybe it is, but you might ask yourself whether such a statement might not also, perfectly appropriately, appear in a guidebook, a piece of tourist talk. Yet as students of the liberal arts, we apparently assume that a historian's way of writing is in some way really different from tourist writing. What is that difference? Is it possible that the mere assigning of a *date* to an event or an object is only the beginning of the historian's task? If so, then what does the rest of his task consist of?

We can begin to suggest some answers to these questions if we read carefully the following piece of historical writing by a recognized historian. Henry Adams, who was a contemporary of Henry James, wrote this description of the towers as part of a famous historical study of the middle ages, *Mont-Saint-Michel and Chartres*. It is not easy reading; there are plenty of names and references you will have to look up in a good encyclopedia. You should also, as you follow Adams' descriptions, refer constantly to the photograph of the cathedral, making sure you can identify the various architectural details that Adams mentions.

The Towers of Chartres

by HENRY ADAMS

For a first visit to Chartres, choose some pleasant morning when the lights are soft, for one wants to be welcome, and the cathedral has moods, at times severe. At best, the Beauce is a country none too gay.

The first glimpse that is caught, and the first that was meant to be caught is that of the two spires. With all the education that Normandy and the Île de France can give, one is still ignorant. The spire is the simplest part of the Romanesque or Gothic architecture, and needs least study in order to be felt. It is a bit of sentiment almost pure of practical purpose. It tells the whole of its story at a glance, and its story is the best that architecture had to tell, for it typified the aspirations of man at the moment when man's aspirations were highest. Yet nine persons out of ten—perhaps ninety-nine in a hundred—who come within sight of the two spires of Chartres will think it a jest if they are told that the smaller of the two, the simpler, the one that impresses them least, is the one which they are expected to recognize as the most perfect piece of architecture in the world. Perhaps the French critics might deny that they make any such absolute claim; in that case you can ask them what their exact claim is; it will always be high enough to astonish the tourist.

Astonished or not, we have got to take this southern spire of the Chartres Cathedral as the object of serious study, and before taking it as art, must take it as history. The foundations of this tower—always to be known as the "old tower"—are supposed to have been laid in 1091, before the first crusade. The flèche was probably half a century later (1145–70). The foundations of the new tower, opposite, were laid not before 1110, when also the portal which stands between them, was begun with the three lancet windows above it, but not the rose. For convenience, this old façade—including the portal and the two towers, but not the flèches, and the three lancet windows, but not the rose—may be dated as complete about 1150.

Originally the whole portal—the three doors and the three lancets—stood nearly forty feet back, on the line of the interior foundations, or rear wall of the towers. This arrangement threw the towers forward, free on three sides, as at Poitiers, and gave room for a parvis, before the portal—a porch, roofed over, to protect the pilgrims who always stopped there to pray before entering the church. When the church was rebuilt after the great fire of 1194, and the architect was required to enlarge the interior, the old portal and lancets were moved bodily forward, to be flush with the front walls of the two towers, as you see the façade today; and the façade itself was heightened, to give room for the rose, and to cover the loftier pignon and vaulting behind. Finally, the wooden roof, above the stone vault, was masked by the Arcade of Kings and its railing, completed in the taste of Philip the Hardy, who reigned from 1270 to 1285.

These changes have, of course, altered the values of all the parts. The portal is injured by being thrown into a glare of light, when it was intended to stand in shadow, as you will see in the north and south porches over the transept portals. The towers are hurt by losing relief and shadow; but the old flèche is obliged to suffer the cruellest wrong of all by having its right shoulder hunched up by half of a huge rose and the whole of a row of kings, when it was built to stand free, and to soar above the whole façade from the top of its second storey. One can easily figure it so and replace the lost parts of the old façade, more or less at haphazard, from the front of Noyon.

What an outrage it was you can see by a single glance at the new flèche opposite. The architect of 1500 has flatly refused to submit to such conditions, and has insisted, with very proper self-respect, on starting from the balustrade of the Arcade of Kings as his level. Not even content with that, he has carried up his square tower another lofty storey before he would consent to touch the heart of his problem, the conversion of the square tower into the octagon flèche. In doing this, he has sacrificed once more the old flèche; but his own tower stands free as it should.

At Vendôme, when you go there, you will be in a way to appreciate still better what happened to the Chartres flèche; for the clocher at Vendôme, which is of the same date—Viollet-le-Duc says earlier, and Enlart, "after 1130"—stood and still stands free, like an Italian campanile, which gives it a vast advantage. The tower of Saint-Leu-d'Esserent, also after 1130, stands free, above the second storey. Indeed, you will hardly find, in the long list of famous French spires, another which has been treated with so much indignity as this, the greatest and most famous of all; and perhaps the most annoying part of it is that you must be grateful to the

architect of 1195 for doing no worse. He has, on the contrary, done
his best to show respect for the work of his predecessor, and has
done so well that, handicapped as it is, the old tower still defies
rivalry. Nearly three hundred and fifty feet high, or, to be exact,
106.5 metres from the church floor, it is built up with an amount
of intelligence and refinement that leaves to unprofessional visitors
no chance to think a criticism—much less to express one. Perhaps—
when we have seen more—and feel less—who knows?—but certainly not now!

"The greatest and surely the most beautiful monument of this
kind that we possess in France," says Viollet-le-Duc; but although
an ignorant spectator must accept the architect's decision on a point
of relative merit, no one is compelled to accept his reasons, as final.
"There is no need to dwell," he continues, "upon the beauty and the
grandeur of composition in which the artist has given proof of rare
sobriety, where all the effects are obtained, not by ornaments, but
by the just and skilful proportion of the different parts. The transition, so hard to adjust, between the square base and the octagon
of the flèche, is managed and carried out with an address which
has not been surpassed in similar monuments." One stumbles a little
at the word "adresse." One never caught one's self using the word in
Norman churches. Your photographs of Bayeux or Boscherville
or Secqueville will show you at a glance whether the term "adresse"
applies to them. Even Vendôme would rather be praised for
"droiture" than for "adresse."—Whether the word "adresse" means
cleverness, dexterity, adroitness, or simple technical skill, the thing
itself is something which the French have always admired more than
the Normans ever did. Viollet-le-Duc himself seems to be a little
uncertain whether to lay most stress on the one or the other quality: "If one tries to appreciate the conception of this tower," quotes
the Abbé Bulteau "one will see that it is as frank as the ex-
ecution is simple and skilful. Starting from the bottom, one reaches
the summit of the flèche without marked break; without anything
to interrupt the general form of the building. This clocher, whose
base is broad (pleine), massive, and free from ornament, transforms
itself, as it springs, into a sharp spire with eight faces, without its

being possible to say where the massive construction ends and the
light construction begins."

.   .   .

One cannot compare Chartres directly with any of its contemporary rivals, but one can at least compare the old spire with the
new one which stands opposite and rises above it. Perhaps you will
like the new best. Built at a time which is commonly agreed to have
had the highest standard of taste, it does not encourage tourist or
artist to insist on setting up standards of his own against it. Begun
in 1507, it was finshed in 1517. The dome of Saint Peter's at Rome,
over which Bramante and Raphael and Michael Angelo toiled, was
building at the same time; Leonardo da Vinci was working at Am-
boise; Jean Bullant, Pierre Lescot, and their patron Francis I, were
beginning their architectural careers. Four hundred years, or there-
abouts, separated the old spire from the new one; and four hundred
more separate the new one from us. If Viollet-le-Duc, who himself
built Gothic spires, had cared to compare his flèches at Clermont-
Ferrand with the new flèche at Chartres, he might perhaps have given
us a rule where "adresse" ceases to have charm, and where detail becomes tiresome; but in the want of a schoolmaster to lay down a law
of taste, you can admire the new flèche as much as you please. Of
course, one sees that the lines of the new tower are not clean, like
those of the old; the devices that cover the transition from the
square to the octagon are rather too obvious; the proportion of the
flèche to the tower quite alters the values of the parts; a rigid classical taste might even go so far as to hint that the new tower, in comparison with the old, showed signs of a certain tendency toward a
dim and distant vulgarity. There can be no harm in admitting that
the new tower is a little wanting in repose for a tower whose business is to counterpoise the very classic lines of the old one; but no
law compels you to insist on absolute repose in any form of art; if
such a law existed, it would have to deal with Michael Angelo
before it dealt with us. The new tower has many faults, but it has
great beauties, as you can prove by comparing it with other late
Gothic spires, including those of Viollet-le-Duc. Its chief fault is to

be where it is. As a companion to the crusades and to Saint Bernard, it lacks austerity. As a companion to the Virgin of Chartres, it recalls Diane de Poitiers.

In fact, the new tower, which in years is four centuries younger than its neighbour, is in feeling fully four hundred years older. It is self-conscious if not vain; its coiffure is elaborately arranged to cover the effects of age, and its neck and shoulders are covered with lace and jewels to hide a certain sharpness of skeleton. Yet it may be beautiful, still; the poets derided the wrinkles of Diane de Poitiers at the very moment when King Henry II idealized her with the homage of a Don Quixote; an atmosphere of physical beauty and decay hangs about the whole Renaissance.

One cannot push these resemblances too far, even for the twelfth century and the old tower. Exactly what date the old tower represents, as a social symbol, is a question that might be as much disputed as the beauty of Diane de Poitiers, and yet half the interest of architecture consists in the sincerity of its reflection of the society that builds. In mere time, by actual date, the old tower represents the second crusade, and when, in 1150, Saint Bernard was elected chief of that crusade in this very cathedral—or rather, in the cathedral of 1120, which was burned—the workmen were probably setting in mortar the stones of the flèche as we now see them; yet the flèche does not represent Saint Bernard in feeling, for Saint Bernard held the whole array of church-towers in horror as signs merely of display, wealth and pride. The flèche rather represents Abbot Suger of Saint-Denis, Abbot Peter the Venerable of Cluny, Abbot Abélard of Saint-Gildas-de-Rhuys, and Queen Eleanor of Guienne, who had married Louis-le-Jeune in 1137; who had taken the cross from Saint Bernard in 1147; who returned from the Holy Land in 1149; and who compelled Saint Bernard to approve her divorce in 1152. Eleanor and Saint Bernard were centuries apart, yet they lived at the same time and in the same church. Speaking exactly, the old tower represents neither of them; the new tower itself is hardly more florid than Eleanor was; perhaps less so, if one can judge from the fashions of the court-dress of her time. The old tower is almost Norman, while Eleanor was wholly Gascon, and Gascony was always florid without being always correct. The new tower, if it had been

built in 1150, like the old one, would have expressed Eleanor perfectly, even in height and apparent effort to dwarf its mate, except
that Eleanor dwarfed her husband without effort, and both in art
and in history the result lacked in harmony.

Be the contrast what it may, it does not affect the fact that no
other church in France has two spires that need be discussed in
comparison with these. Indeed, no other cathedral of the same class
has any spires at all, and this superiority of Chartres gave most of
its point to a saying that "with the spires of Chartres, the choir of
Beauvais, the nave of Amiens, and the façade of Rheims," one could
make a perfect church—for us tourists.

It is true, after all, that one thing a historian clearly does, and
that Henry Adams does too, is assign dates to things. He gives
us plain "facts," and in this respect he writes at times like a particularly thorough tourist handbook or an encyclopedia. Thus
Adams' third paragraph is devoted simply to dating the old
tower (1091–1170) and the old part of the façade generally
("about 1150"). Here is information for us to note down and
commit to memory if we like. But the question we have been
asking is: What else does a good historian do? Does he *see* his
world simply as a series of identifications in a chronological number system, or are the relations he is interested in more complicated than that?

It would be a mistake, of course, to generalize about all good
historians from this passage by Adams, but at least we can say
what Adams does with his terms besides mere dating. Before
we try to define what that is, we had better make sure we know
at least some of Adams' names and dates. On the next page is a
scheme with some information we need to have.

Now what does Adams make of these names and dates that
might go beyond the simple assigning of numbers to people or
objects? First, and very important, he *looks* with great care at
the two towers, and uses his looking to make further relations.
We can see what sort of relations these are by studying his elabo-

CATHEDRAL OF NOTRE-DAME AT CHARTRES

NEW OR NORTH TOWER	OLD OR SOUTH TOWER
(on left in photograph)	(on right in photograph)
constructed 1507–1517 Henry II, born 1519; King of France, 1547–59	constructed 1091–1170 Saint Bernard, 1090?–1153; preached Second Crusade
Diane de Poitiers, 1499–1566, mistress of Henry II with strong political influence over him	Eleanor of Aquitaine, 1122?–1204, queen of Louis VII of France, later of Henry II of England, strong-minded politically able, patroness of courtly literature and art

rate contrast between the two towers in the last four paragraphs of the passage. He begins by giving each tower a character, a personality, a "feeling" that is derived from his own contemplation of details of the two structures. This feeling is outside of time—it is any time. "One sees that the lines of the new tower are not clean, like those of the old; the devices that cover the transition from the square to the octagon are rather too obvious." (Can *you* see these things, on the photograph?) There is even, he hints, "a certain tendency toward a dim and distant vulgarity." Here we can see the early stages of a metaphor that Adams is going to develop at some length—namely, the new tower seen as a person, specifically as a woman, a sort of royal whore. The tower has "great beauties," but "its chief fault is to be where it is. As a companion to the crusades and to Saint Bernard, it lacks austerity." The crusades and the saintly Bernard, of course, were contemporaries of the *old* tower, of which the new one is such an uncomfortable "companion." "As a companion to the Virgin of Chartres, it recalls Diane de Poitiers."

We all know who the Virgin was, and we can begin to see why

Adams considers the new tower rather too vulgar for her. But
who was Diane de Poitiers? If you knew nothing about her but
her dates (contemporary with the new tower), you could perhaps learn almost all you needed to know from the next paragraph. The new tower, though younger "in years," is older "in
feeling," and Diane de Poitiers, vain and powerful mistress of
Henry II, becomes for Adams a *term* with which to *see* the feeling of the tower. The metaphor proceeds: "It is self-conscious
if not vain; its coiffure is elaborately arranged to cover the effects
of age, and its neck and shoulders are covered with lace and
jewels to hide a certain sharpness of skeleton." You might try to
see some of these things for yourself in the photograph: coiffure,
lace and jewels, sharpness of skeleton. You might also note in
our list of dates that Diane de Poitiers was born twenty years
before her royal lover; she must have been able to "cover the
effects of age" with considerable skill.

So much then for the new tower, which is defined not only
chronologically but also "in feeling," by becoming associated
metaphorically with a famous woman of the time who offers a
useful way of seeing this piece of architecture. The old tower
proves to be more difficult. "Yet half the interest of architecture
consists in the sincerity of its reflection of the society that builds,"
so we try as we can to *characterize* this tower in the same way,
by associating it with a contemporary figure. It doesn't work.
Saint Bernard won't do; he was too pure even for this purest of
churches. Queen Eleanor of Guienne (or Aquitaine) is suggested, the most powerful and energetic woman of the time. But
she won't do either, being far too "florid" a figure for the simplicity of the old tower. "Speaking exactly, the old tower represents neither of them." It defies this sort of analysis, perhaps, in
the way that the whole façade seemed to defy James.

At this point we might pause to ask what it means, in Adams'
sense here, to "speak exactly." To speak exactly is to speak of
more than dates. Obviously, if mere dating were the whole issue,

then a label like "mid-twelfth-century" would satisfactorily
"cover" Saint Bernard, Eleanor, and the old tower, all three.
But for Adams such a label is by itself nowhere near satisfactory.
A lot of other distinctions are at stake: aesthetic ones about architecture, and moral ones about people in history. "Eleanor and
Saint Bernard were centuries apart, yet they lived at the same
time and in the same church." The double use Adams makes of
time is nowhere more evident than in this sentence. They lived
at the same time *in years,* but they were centuries apart *in feeling.*
And now Adams turns things around to some extent, by using a
vocabulary of time to describe someone who did *not* live in that
time. Eleanor, he says (to "speak exactly"), was like the *new*
tower, like the mid-sixteenth century, four hundred years after
her actual life span. So finally, in this brand of history, a whole
period is given a kind of personality, a feeling. While he makes
these vast relations, however, the tone of the author's voice, which
has many touches of easy informality, reminds us not to take
these equations as God-given truths, but as one man's way of
coming to *terms* with the past.

Adams concludes the passage with a reference to "us tourists,"
an example of this easy tone. From what we have just observed,
you may conclude that this is another mask, a self-consciously
modest pose, like Mark Twain's posture of ignorance in Theme
3. Adams too is certainly no ordinary tourist; in fact he is hardly
a tourist at all. Instead, he is using language as a particularly
imaginative and sensitive historical writer, and that is the leap
you are asked to take in composing Theme 9.

DIRECTIONS FOR THEME 9

GO BACK TO THE CHURCH WHOSE FAÇADE YOU DESCRIBED IN
THEME 8, AND RESEE THAT FAÇADE IN LANGUAGE A HISTORIAN

MIGHT USE. YOU MAY UNDERTAKE ALL THE RESEARCH YOU
WANT, AS TO DATES AND SO ON, BUT YOUR SUCCESS WILL DE-
PEND NOT ON THE ACCURACY OF A SET OF GUIDEBOOK FACTS,
BUT ON YOUR ABILITY TO RECREATE THIS FAÇADE THROUGH
APPROPRIATE USE OF HISTORICAL METAPHOR.

10

HISTORY AS WAYS OF LOOKING

The practical requirements which underlie every historical judgment give to all history the character of "contemporary history" because, however remote in time events there recounted may seem to be, the history in reality refers to present needs and present situations wherein those events vibrate.

—CROCE

The article that follows was written by a young man who at the time of writing was a teacher of history at Columbia. He considers here some of the difficulties that confront the historian, and he begins with a question—"What is a historical fact?" As usual, your problem is to relate the words of this article to your own experience as an amateur writer of history yourself. As you study the article, therefore, keep before you your own Theme 9, and try to find in your own writing some examples of problems the article discusses. A few of its key terms are: historical fact, frame of reference or theory of history, cause, relativity of history. Your task in Theme 10, then, will be to scrutinize your own language in relation to some of these words and phrases.

The Relativity of History

by CHARLES WOOLSEY COLE

The question arises, "What is a historical fact?" The answer is
that it is, at its best, what the historian thinks of what some one
else thinks he saw or said or did or heard. At its worst it is a paltry
third or fourth-hand judgment. Psychology will have to develop
much further before it can be known what relation something which
has passed through the central neural processes of at least two men
has to any objective reality. Still, such "facts" are at their simplest
fairly clear-cut. The more they deal with complex situations, with
motives, causes, effects, changes or connections, the more nebulous
they become. But that is not all, for the very simplest and clearest
historical fact, when isolated, has little meaning. It has to be tied
to other facts to bring out its importance. When, however, it comes
to a question of selecting, relating and ordering facts, history becomes essentially subjective. In short, the relation between any page
of history and some objective reality which once existed is tenuous.
The meaning and significance of that page are in large part, at
least, the results of subjective processes of the historian's mind. With
all the will to objectivity in the world, with all the honesty that can
be conceived, with all the desire to tell things exactly as they happened, the historian cannot produce work which has at the same
time significance and a close relationship to something that ob-
jectively existed in the past. . . .

The historical fact, *in itself*, has little significance. . . . If a frame
of reference can be discovered and the historical fact related to it,
perhaps the fact will be clothed in a new meaning. That is just what
historians have always tended to do, for it is a commonplace that
every age writes its own history according to its own beliefs and
ideas. From the beginning of the Christian era well into the seven-

From "The Relativity of History" in *Political Science Quarterly*, XLVIII,
2 (June, 1933). Reprinted by permission of the *Quarterly* and the author.

teenth century, from Orosius to Cotton Mather, historians took their material and related it to their theories of a divine order, of the workings of God upon man, of man's search for eternal salvation. So related, facts were significant, and if an earthquake became a judgment of God, still the history as a whole had a meaning. In the eighteenth century historians related their facts to theories as to the rational order of nature, natural laws, the rights of man or the like. In the nineteenth century they gave their facts meaning by tying them to nationalist, democratic, socialist or evolutionary theories.

Today either historians give their facts significance by using explicitly one of the older theories, as Spengler has used and strained the biologic analogy; or other and perhaps newer theories are implicit in their work. They seek for objectivity, but they must select and order and interpret the facts. This they can do fairly and justly but they cannot do it without some theories in the light of which they may select and order and interpret. What is the social order and economic history of the present but history written under the influence of theories as to the paramount importance of the evolution of social and economic institutions and folkways? If the modern social historian could present his arguments to the Venerable Bede, that worthy might well shrug his shoulders and reply, "To me these things that you call social and economic are all very well, but I wish to see how it was that God ordained the conversion of the British Isles."

Historical facts, then, gain their meaning when by order, selection and interpretation they are related to a frame of reference. This frame of reference is a theory of, or a way of looking at history, explicit or implicit, old or new. Without relation to some theory the fact is an isolated entity of dubious validity and little meaning. Without some theory the historian cannot, from the immense mass of historical facts, select and order his material, or interpret what he has chosen and arranged. . . .

The remark is often heard, "We shall have to wait for the judgment of history on that", or "We are so close to this that we cannot write the history of it; we shall have to wait until time has given us the proper perspective." Such statements do not mean that con-

temporaries who share in events and know at least something of
their psychological bases would not be the best ones to write the
history of the era. Nor does it mean that the historian must wait
hungrily until some government sees fit to disgorge a few incrimi-
nating documents, or until some statesman takes his pen in hand to
write an unreliable apologia. They mean that the contemporary can
see sequence but not causes. To write of causes the historian must
wait until the material has shaken down into patterns, patterns not
inherent in the events but arising gradually from the minds of men
who in after years think about the events. While the historian waits
for the formation of these patterns, the *Zeitgeist* dissolves, most of
the material is lost and buried. But the historian must wait, for
until the patterns, or theories of causation, are built up out of the
scattered fragments of an era he cannot write intelligible history
which shows events proceeding from cause to effect. Events are
linked in time and space, but the causal connections between them
are evolved from the subjective processes of men who think about
them.

The very idea of causation is injected from without into an in-
coherent mass of chance-ordained events by the historian's processes of selection, ordering and interpretation. Causes in written
history proceed not from any objective reality on which the writing
is based, but from a subjective adherence by the historian to some
theory or frame of reference to which he can relate his facts. Yet
the historian should not flinch before the idea that the material
with which he deals is in actuality chance-ordained, when it is
becoming more apparent all the time that the basic processes of
nature must be described in terms of chance and not of mechanical
determinism. . . .

If, then, the significance of historical facts—and the same reasoning might be applied to the data of the other social sciences—
together with their causal connections and their continuity proceed
from their being related to some frame of reference, which is to
say some implicit or explicit theory, the position of a theory in history becomes quite different. In the past theories have been tested
by the supposedly empirical method of referring them to the "facts
of history", that is, by referring them to rather misty entities which

take on meaning, continuity, or connection only in the light of the theories themselves. If it should happen that the new point of view based on hints from the recent work in the physical sciences should come to be adopted, the theories of history would be placed consciously in a respectable and stable position. No longer would they cringe and cower like handmaidens before the queenly "facts". For they would be tested not only by the facts, but by pragmatic criteria as to whether they served their purpose of giving in abundance to the facts of history significance, connection and continuity, as to whether they became the foci of broad syntheses which tended from a practical and from a pedagogic point of view to make history intelligible and valuable, and finally as to whether they conformed to similar theories in other fields of knowledge.

Practically, the adoption of such an attitude toward their material would mean that thinkers in history would in part turn their attention from delving after facts to an effort to build up theories and philosophies. As the work progressed theories would come and go and change, but gradually there might arise magnificent beacons in whose light human history would glow with renewed beauty, enhanced significance, close-knit interconnection and intelligible causality.

When, in Theme 9, you saw your church façade as a historian might see it, you could have interpreted your "historical facts" in any of a wide variety of ways. Yet if Mr. Cole's argument is a fair one, you could not have interpreted your facts without making use, perhaps unconsciously, of a "frame of reference" or "theory" of history. What is such a frame of reference? It is, Cole states, "a way of looking at history, explicit or implicit, old or new," and historians simply cannot operate "without some theories *in the light of which* they may select and order and interpret." (You observe that this article, like many other passages in this book, makes repeated use of "looking" and "light" as metaphors for intellectual activity; the beacons in the final sentence are a shining example.) Now the question is, what par-

ticular "light" did you make use of in Theme 9, in order
to "look" at your church façade in historical terms? For
example, let us suppose that your church was of the puri-
tan-New England sort, all clapboards and white pillars. You
might have seen its façade, then, as simple and chaste, a maidenly
expression of an uncomplicated faith with no sophisticated refine-
ments or adornments. In that case you would be making a causal
relation between a spiritual attitude (puritan simplicity and
rigor) and an architectural form (clapboards and white pillars).
And the light, the frame of reference or theory you would be
drawing on would be one of *religious* history. But how easily you
might have chosen some other light to illuminate some other relation. You could have turned yourself into an *economic* historian,
for example, with quite a different theory of causation. The church
in this case would be seen, not as a chaste and pious maiden, but
as a practical barnlike structure of some crudity, and you would
account for this by pointing not to religious beliefs, but to such
"facts" as the lack of good masons in early New England, the
abundance of forests for building materials, and the financial
necessity of making do with an unadorned and inexpensive building. Why, finally, you choose the religious theory or the economic
theory or some other as your favorite "light," the one you would
be most disposed to see by and defend, is a question that can
probably be answered only by the strictest introspection into your
own values and thought processes.

DIRECTIONS FOR THEME 10

SELECT A STATEMENT FROM YOUR THEME 9 IN WHICH YOU EX-
PRESSED OR IMPLIED A CAUSAL RELATION BETWEEN HISTORICAL
"FACTS." SHOW JUST WHAT RELATION YOU WERE MAKING:
WHAT FACT CAUSED WHAT OTHER FACT? THEN SHOW WHAT
FRAME OF REFERENCE OR THEORY OF HISTORY IS SUGGESTED BY
THE PARTICULAR RELATION YOU MADE. WHAT OTHER THEORY

OF HISTORY MIGHT HAVE PROMPTED SOME OTHER CAUSAL RELA-
TION BETWEEN THE SAME TWO FACTS? ILLUSTRATE THIS OTHER
POSSIBILITY IN DETAIL, AND THEN SHOW, IF YOU CAN, WHY YOU
CHOSE ORIGINALLY THE PARTICULAR FRAME OF REFERENCE YOU
DID RATHER THAN SOME OTHER.

11

SEEING THE WIND

*The wind bloweth where it listeth, and thou
hearest the sound thereof, but canst not tell
whence it cometh, and whither it goeth.*

—JOHN, 3:8

In Theme 11 you are asked to "see" something that strictly
speaking cannot be seen at all—the wind. The sensation of observing the wind is an everyday occurrence in your life. Can you
say what it is like?

It is probably unlikely that reading three poems about the
wind will give you any help at all in fulfilling this assignment.
On the other hand reading poems never hurt anybody. Here for
your pleasure is a literary fling at the wind, to use as you will
or can.

from Prothalamion

by EDMUND SPENSER

Calme was the day, and through the trembling ayre
Sweet-breathing Zephyrus did softly play,
A gentle spirit, that lightly did delay
Hot Titans beames, which then did glyster fayre;

When I, (whom sullein care,
Through discontent of my long fruitlesse stay
In Princes Court, and expectation vayne
Of idle hopes, which still doe fly away,
Like empty shadowes, did afflict my brayne,)
Walkt forth to ease my payne
Along the shoare of silver streaming Themmes;
Whose rutty Bancke, the which his River hemmes,
Was paynted all with variable flowers,
And all the meades adornd with daintie gemmes,
Fit to decke maydens bowres,
And crowne their Paramours
Against the Brydale day, which is not long:
  Sweete Themmes! runne softly, till I end my Song.

Ode to the West Wind

by PERCY BYSSHE SHELLEY

I

O wild West Wind, thou breath of Autumn's being,
Thou, from whose unseen presence the leaves dead
Are driven, like ghosts from an enchanter fleeing,

Yellow, and black, and pale, and hectic red,
Pestilence-stricken multitudes: O thou
Who chariotest to their dark wintry bed

The wingéd seeds, where they lie cold and low,
Each like a corpse within its grave, until
Thine azure sister of the Spring shall blow

Her clarion o'er the dreaming earth, and fill
(Driving sweet buds like flocks to feed in air)
With living hues and odours plain and hill:

Wild Spirit, which art moving everywhere;
Destroyer and Preserver; hear, oh, hear!

II

Thou on whose stream, mid the steep sky's commotion,
Loose clouds like earth's decaying leaves are shed,
Shook from the tangled boughs of Heaven and Ocean,

Angels of rain and lightning: there are spread
On the blue surface of thine airy surge,
Like the bright hair uplifted from the head

Of some fierce Maenad, even from the dim verge
Of the horizon to the zenith's height,
The locks of the approaching storm. Thou dirge

Of the dying year, to which this closing night
Will be the dome of a vast sepulchre,
Vaulted with all thy congregated might

Of vapours, from whose solid atmosphere
Black rain, and fire, and hail, will burst: oh, hear!

III

Thou who didst waken from his summer dreams
The blue Mediterranean, where he lay,
Lulled by the coil of his crystalline streams,

Beside a pumice isle in Baiae's bay,
And saw in sleep old palaces and towers
Quivering within the wave's intenser day,

All overgrown with azure moss and flowers
So sweet, the sense faints picturing them! Thou
For whose path the Atlantic's level powers

Cleave themselves into chasms, while far below
The sea-blooms and the oozy woods which wear
The sapless foliage of the ocean, know

Thy voice, and suddenly grow gray with fear,
And tremble and despoil themselves: oh, hear!

IV

If I were a dead leaf thou mightest bear;
If I were a swift cloud to fly with thee;
A wave to pant beneath thy power, and share

The impulse of thy strength, only less free
Than thou, O uncontrollable! If even
I were as in my boyhood, and could be

The comrade of thy wanderings over Heaven,
As then, when to outstrip the skyey speed
Scarce seemed a vision; I would ne'er have striven

As thus with thee in prayer in my sore need.
Oh, lift me as a wave, a leaf, a cloud!
I fall upon the thorns of life! I bleed!

A heavy weight of hours has chained and bowed
One too like thee: tameless, and swift, and proud.

V

Make me thy lyre, even as the forest is:
What if my leaves are falling like its own!
The tumult of they mighty harmonies

Will take from both a deep, autumnal tone,
Sweet though in sadness. Be thou, Spirit fierce,
My spirit! Be thou me, impetuous one!

Drive my dead thought over the universe
Like withered leaves to quicken a new birth!
And, by the incantation of this verse,

Scatter, as from an unextinguished hearth
Ashes and sparks, my words among mankind!
Be through my lips to unawakened earth

The trumpet of a prophecy! O Wind,
If Winter comes, can Spring be far behind?

Why east wind chills

by DYLAN THOMAS

Why east wind chills and south wind cools
Shall not be known till windwell dries
And west's no longer drowned
In winds that bring the fruit and rind
Of many a hundred falls;
Why silk is soft and the stone wounds
The child shall question all his days,
Why night-time rain and the breast's blood
Both quench his thirst he'll have a black reply.

When cometh Jack Frost? the children ask.
Shall they clasp a comet in their fists?
Not till, from high and low, their dust
Sprinkles in children's eyes a long-last sleep
And dusk is crowded with the children's ghosts,
Shall a white answer echo from the rooftops.

All things are known: the stars' advice
Calls some content to travel with the winds,
Though what the stars ask as they round
Time upon time the towers of the skies
Is heard but little till the stars go out.
I hear content, and 'Be content'
Ring like a handbell through the corridors,
And 'Know no answer,' and I know
No answer to the children's cry
Of echo's answer and the man of frost
And ghostly comets over the raised fists.

DIRECTIONS FOR THEME I I

TAKE A STAND AT A PARTICULAR PLACE AND TIME, AND DESCRIBE
THE WIND JUST AS THOROUGHLY AS YOU CAN. TRY IT IN VERSE
IF YOU LIKE.

12

WIND AS SCIENCE

The world is in a constant flux around and in us, but in order to grapple with the floating reality we create in our thought, or at any rate in our language, certain more or less fixed points, certain averages. Reality never presents us with an average but language does.

—OTTO JESPERSON

Of course there are a thousand ways to see the wind. You can even talk to it—"O wild West Wind," cries Shelley. The terms available for describing the wind are practically infinite, and one reason for this may be, as we have already pointed out, that you can't see wind at all, directly. All you can do is sense it through signs: rustling of leaves, blowing of smoke, cool sensation on your face. You interpret certain feelings that your senses give you, and you call that wind. To recall the language of Theme 3, you observe the world around you and *read* it as wind.

In this next exercise you are going to try to see wind in one particular set of terms—the terms of numbers. To see things as numbers, to "measure" things, is a way of seeing that enjoys enormous prestige in our time, and it suggests all the dramatic improvements of life that have accompanied the growth of science. Whatever else it is that scientists do, one thing they obviously do is measure things, so that the world becomes defined in relation to an organization of statistical language.

How can you express the wind statistically? You have to have a device, an instrument of some sort, and in the case of measuring the speed of the wind, this instrument is called an anemometer. Then you communicate your various readings of this instrument by making use of a scale of measurement. Here, for example, is a famous scale of measurement—one invented by an Admiral Beaufort in 1806. As you study it, try to determine what instrument Beaufort has selected for his readings. What was Beaufort's anemometer?

Beaufort Number	Description of the Wind	Beaufort's Criteria	
0	Calm		
1	Light Air	Just sufficient to give steerage way	
2	Light Breeze	with which a well-conditioned	1 to 2 knots
3	Gentle Breeze	man-of-war under all sail, and	3 to 4 knots
4	Moderate Breeze	clean full, would go in smooth	5 to 6 knots
		water from	
5	Fresh Breeze		Royals, etc.
6	Strong Breeze	in which the same	Single-reefs & topgallants
7	Moderate Gale	ship could just	Double-reefs, jibs, etc.
8	Fresh Gale	carry close hauled	Triple-reefs, courses, etc.
9	Strong Gale		Close-reefs and courses
10	Whole Gale	with which she could only bear close-reefed main topsail and reefed foresail.	
11	Storm	with which she could be reduced to storm staysails.	
12	Hurricane	to which she could show no canvas.	

Beaufort's anemometer was of course "a well-conditioned man-of-war," with all her complications of sails and rigging. That is the instrument he reads with this scale. For example, if the wind were blowing so hard that such a ship could just carry close-hauled single reefs and topgallants, then we are to name that

wind a "Strong Breeze" or Beaufort 6. And what is the advantage
of such naming? One advantage you can readily appreciate simply by casting your eye down the left-hand row of numbers and
comparing their brevity with the vastly more cumbersome phras-
ing under the headings "Description of the Wind" and "Beaufort's Criteria." The numbers are so simple! They are so easy to
tell to someone else, so easy for a ship captain to enter in his log.
Yet they are also, perhaps you will want to object, *too* simple.
"Beaufort 6" is not an adequate translation of "Strong breeze in
which a well-conditioned man-of-war could just carry close-
hauled single-reefs and topgallants." To this objection one can
only say that this always happens when life is expressed in statistics, or indeed any simple terms. There is a great gain in ease of
communication; there is a great loss in richness and precision.
Notice the paradox that numbers are actually *im*precise, inasmuch as they fail to show the indefiniteness of actual experience.
This is a constant problem in science, and it occurs in all acts of
measurement, even when the instrument being read and recorded
with pencil and paper is, say, a needle on a dial, and not a well-
conditioned man-of-war. The physicist, P. W. Bridgman, has put
it this way: "Any physical indefiniteness does not get into the
paper and pencil operations because the first preliminary to the
paper and pencil operations is to replace the instrumental indi-
cations by numbers mathematically sharp." The sharpness, then,
the clarity and simplicity, are in the mathematics, not in the
wind. It would be hard to overemphasize this truth.

Now how can you proceed as a scientist, however amateur,
and see wind numerically? You will need an anemometer, and
you will not find it convenient to use a well-conditioned man-of-
war. You will have to make your own instrument, and invent a
scale of measurement to use with it. Your terms will not be
"Beaufort 1–2–3," or miles per hour, but your own: "Smith
1–2–3," "O'Callahan 1–2–3." Before going ahead with this
project it will be helpful for you to read a few pages from a stand-

ard meteorological text of some years ago in which wind and various methods and difficulties of measuring it are discussed.

Wind

by SIR NAPIER SHAW

The chief element in the structure of the atmosphere is the wind, the motion of the air. It is also the most difficult to visualise from fixed instruments, designed for the express purpose, under the general name of anemometers, because all such instruments have to be attached to some structure. Within the limit of height of all solid structures the motion of the air is complicated by the eddies due to what is called the friction of the ground, partly the actual resistance of fixed obstacles, hills, buildings, trees, etc., or moving obstacles, waves of water, etc., and partly to the molecular viscosity of the air which would still produce some effect even if the surface of the land or sea were perfectly level. . . . The layer of the atmosphere near the surface, where instruments for measuring the direction and velocity of the wind are of necessity installed, is most unsatisfactory for the purpose, and this opinion is amply justified by the extraordinary complication which the records of any anemometer disclose. Some are more complicated than others but all show some degree of complication, and the problem of obtaining an idea of the changes of the general atmospheric structure from the records of an anemometer is a very awkward one.

The number of anemometers designed for measuring or recording the direction and velocity of the wind is very large. . . . Meteorological practice has in the course of time concentrated its attention on two forms of anemometer, the Robinson anemometer which consists of horizontal cross-arms with hemispherical cups at their ends, the rate of rotation of which is very nearly proportional to the "mean" velocity of the wind, and the Dines anemograph which,

From *Manual of Meteorology,* Vols. I and IV, copyright, 1926–30, by Sir Napier Shaw. Reprinted by permission of Cambridge University Press.

like the Pitot tube, depends upon the pressure exerted by the wind upon the opening of a tube. It is measured by some form of pressure-gauge always with the proviso that since a pressure-gauge has two openings, one for each side of the gauge, the instruments must make due allowance for the effect of the wind upon the second limb of the gauge. . . .

[Another] method of recording the force and direction of the wind is by means of a plate which is turned by a vane to face the wind and which records the force by the compression of a spring. This plan is used in Osler's anemometer which has been in continuous operation at the Royal Observatory, Greenwich, since January 13, 1841. The records are published in the reports of the Observatory.

They ought to show a relation with the records of the Robinson anemograph not differing much from:

$$F = .003V^2,$$

where F is the pressure in lbs. per sq. ft. and V the velocity in miles per hour. They do not do so. The differences may perhaps be accounted for by the fact that the plate would adjust its record to the extremes of a transient gust and the anemograph shows only the smoothed value. But that is only a partial explanation, the differences are too great. One of the curiosities of meteorological work upon wind is that differences of the kind here referred to are tolerated for years without anyone feeling it necessary to explore the subject to the point of actual conviction.

The secret of that really intolerable toleration is the basic difficulty of all anemographic records—the exposure. The reading of any anemograph is a function not only of the instrument but of the site, and of the shape and orientation of the structure upon which the instrument is mounted. Any flat vertical surface exposed to the wind produces a localised eddy analogous to what is treated elsewhere as a cliff-eddy, and a few degrees of difference in the orientation of the wind may have a considerable effect on the record. The conclusion arrived at in the Meteorological Office was that nothing short of a separate structure, a tower of open ironwork, on a very open space of level ground was really efficient and even in that case

. . . distant geographical features may have a paramount influence upon the record of the wind. . . .

Hence it has come about that unless the local opportunity for exposure was exceptionally good it was not thought desirable to insist upon, or even to advise, the erection of an elaborate instrument for recording the wind. Wind did not really lend itself to recording, except in a specially local sense, local as to building as well as site and general locality. It was thought better to get the general impression of the wind which is expressed by the adaptation of the Beaufort scale to observations on land than to obtain a more precise numerical value which had to meteorological significance of the same order of accuracy. No structure of meteorological reasoning can be raised without a tolerance of at least 20 per cent. in the assigned values of surface-winds.

The reader may be surprised to learn that measuring the wind is really a most difficult operation, but he may realise the truth of the statement when he understands that thirty years ago, on account of the inherent difficulty of the subject, the Meteorological Office has to be content to publish values of wind-velocity which were known to be in error by 25 per cent., and even now the quotation, without reference, of a reading of an anemometer from a considerable number of meteorological publications is no guarantee that an error of that order of magnitude is not involved. By the turn of the century much had been done and the accuracy of wind measurements has been still further improved in recent years by the use of wind-channels set up for aeronautical investigations. In working conditions an ordinary measure of wind as represented on a weather-map of the British Isles and the neighboring parts of the continent and the islands of the Atlantic is obtained for the most part by estimation according to the Beaufort scale, and the same is true universally of the measures of wind at sea which are generally available for meteorological study. In order to express these estimates in terms of velocity the equivalents of the numbers of the Beaufort scale are employed. The scale was obtained by taking the mean value of many individual observations which show very considerable diversity among themselves and, strictly speaking, it can only be regarded as applicable when in like manner the means of a large number of estimates are under consideration. Any individual estimate of wind-force is liable to the various causes, partly peculiar to the locality or the special conditions of weather and partly personal to the observer, which account for the large range of estimates included under the same number of the scale in the formation of the table of equivalents. At a few observatories measures of the wind for use in the preparation of weather-maps are obtained by anemometers and the figures are transformed into the numbers of the Beaufort scale for transmission by telegraph by the use of the same table of equivalents. In such cases there are no uncertainties in the measurement such as are inseparable from personal estimates but the peculiarities of the exposure of the anemometers are at present even more disturbing than the vagueness of personal estimates. The older observatories were provided with recording cup-anemometers of the Robinson type and these are very heavy instruments which have to be supported on substantial structures and are generally installed on large buildings which, with their surroundings, affect the flow of air past the instrument with eddies of various kinds. The subject is at present not at all fully investigated and it has only recently been pointed out in a summary of the occurrence of gales in various localities that, for this reason, the observatories of the Meteorological Office are characterised by a singular and anomolous freedom from gales which is really attributable to the exposure of the anemometers.

.   .   .   .   .   .

GUSTINESS AND EDDIES

When the tube-anemometer, devised by W. H. Dines in 1890, was set in operation the wind was seen from the records to consist of a series of rapid alternations of velocity, and when a direction-recorder was subsequently added the alternations in velocity were found to be accompanied by corresponding alternations in direction.

We have stated the general problem of the meteorological calculus as being the interpretation of the record of a pressure-tube anemometer with the understanding that the incidents of history recorded in the trace, in so far as they can be regarded as referring to entities with a certain validity, are probably the result of some analogy in the local motion of the air to the rotation of a solid. We may recognise something which bears out this suggestion in shiftiness, in gustiness, in squalls, whirlwinds and tornadoes, and the suggestions of revolving fluid to be found in the isobars of weather-maps.

Our first business is with the gustiness and shiftiness which is the common characteristic of anemometer records when there is a reasonable flow.

It is agreed that the gustiness so recorded is due to turbulence: that turbulence is eddy-motion treated statistically, quite unrestricted as to the three dimensions, horizontal and vertical; and that an eddy represents the effort of spin to preserve the identity of the parcel of air which has been made to spin with some analogy to a revolving solid by the interference of an obstacle of some sort with the steady flow of current.

Anemograph records make it quite clear that the effect of the eddies which are expressed statistically as turbulence is of the same order of magnitude as the flow, sometimes annihilating it or even reversing it and sometimes doubling its speed. . . .

A permanent eddy is formed at the edges of cliffs or the ridges of houses or walls in all strong winds. The reader can make experiments for himself, simply with an empty match box or even his own hat, in the eddy formed by a strong wind blowing upon a nearly vertical cliff. A most remarkable example of a cliff-eddy can be found at the Rock of Gibraltar when a strong levanter blows on the steep eastern face of the Rock. Its effect upon the tube-anemometer which was maintained at the signal station on the Rock was very remarkable. When the velocity of the wind reached a certain limit it passed the opening of the anemometer in a direction nearly vertical and the effect was a reduction of the pressure in the recording float. A limit is thus fixed to the velocity which the instrument can record and gusts of greater velocity appear on the record as entirely fictitious lulls, due to the withdrawal of the pen to the zero line by the "suction" of the air passing the anemometer.

As Sir Napier says, "measuring the wind is really a most difficult operation." Now try it.

DIRECTIONS FOR THEME 12

BUILD YOUR OWN ANEMOMETER. USE PAPER CLIPS, CARDBOARD, PENCIL STUBS, SLICED PINGPONG BALLS, WHATEVER YOUR INGENUITY CAN DEVISE. WRITE A CAREFUL ACCOUNT OF HOW YOU BUILT YOUR ANEMOMETER. THEN RUN A SERIES OF TESTS WITH IT, USING A SCALE OF MEASUREMENT OF YOUR OWN INVENTION. DESCRIBE THESE TESTS. WHAT WOULD YOU SAY WAS SCIENTIFIC ABOUT THIS EXPERIENCE? WHAT WAS NOT SCIENTIFIC?

13

THE HUMAN
STANDPOINT

Go, wondrous creature! mount where Science guides,
Go, measure earth, weigh air, and state the tides.

—POPE

The author of the following article on the "revolution" in modern physics is not a professional scientist—he is a professor of English. In the book from which this passage is taken, called *Science and Criticism*, Mr. Muller presents himself as a "layman" or even as a "literary fellow." He is consciously concerned, therefore, with making connections between science and other "lay" areas of activity, and that, of course, is one of the principal aims of a liberal arts student in becoming acquainted with scientific ways of doing things.

You have just completed a modest experience in a kind of scientific activity—measuring the wind. As you read this article, try to make its terms relevant to your recent experience. No one would want to say that your homemade anemometer and a physicist's latest atom-smasher are in most senses comparable instruments. Still, your situation as a measurer of wind was not so

thoroughly remote from the situation of serious scientists as you
may have supposed.

The Revolution in Physics

by HERBERT J. MULLER

"See Mystery to Mathematics fly!" wrote Pope in a simpler age.
Today the layman who attempts to follow the flight through the
probability waves in the time-space continuum is apt to appreciate
the blessed old mysteries. The chief trouble is that he really wants
to *see*. He lives in a commonsense world full of material things and
uses a language full of nouns, which by definition are "substantives"
or names of these things. Stubbornly he asks, What *is* an electromagnetic field? what *is* a line of force? To such questions physicists
are blandly indifferent. They still tolerate "matter" but only on
sufferance; many look forward to a day in which they can dispense
with this "theoretical construction" and explain everything in terms
of "field"—although this too is not necessarily "real." In general,
they do not care what their symbols "stand for" so long as they can
get handier equations. Space has the physical property of transmit-
ting electromagnetic waves, Einstein tells us, and we should not
"bother too much about the meaning of this statement."

Yet one need not fly all the way to mathematics to catch the main
idea of what is going on—the specific equations will probably have
been revised before he has got to them anyway. The permanent
contribution of modern physics lies in its new base of operations.
Between the calculations of Newton and Einstein there is only a
slight difference; for all ordinary purposes one can still measure
things in the old-time way. Between the implications of their theories, however, there is an enormous difference. And this difference,
in which lies the profoundest revolution of an age noisy with revolu-
tions, the layman can grasp.

In its main outlines, the story of what has happened is familiar enough. Classical physics explained everything in terms of matter and motion in Euclidean space, running the ancient forms of Being by as immutable a clockwork mechanism. From the beginning there were troublesome fictions, such as the apparently jelly-like "ether" that transmitted light but somehow offered no resistance to the wheeling spheres; yet the whole scheme was built solidly on common sense, and it seemed to work beautifully. The first principles of physics were accordingly regarded as a priori, its framework and method as inevitable and inalterable. Jealous philosophers kept raising questions, asking how our senses enabled us to be so intimate with the little lumps of matter and how these lumps kept pushing one another around, but the very success of scientists resulted from their indifference to such questions, their naïve acceptance of a faith without bothering to explain or justify it. In time, however, they accumulated more and more experimental data—especially regarding electricity—that could not be explained satisfactorily by their mechanistic concepts. Clerk Maxwell's brilliant electromagnetic theory of light did *not* have a mechanical basis, yet it also seemed to work. Hence their very successes finally forced scientists to look to their faith. And even as Renan was exclaiming, "The world today has no more mysteries!" this tidy world was crumbling.

The story may conveniently begin with one of the greatest but least known of Russian revolutionists, the mathematician Lobachevsky. Euclid's axiom, that through a given point only one parallel could be drawn to a given line, had been considered a fact of nature, plain to the eye. But in 1826 Lobachevsky, as if just for the hell of it, denied this self-evident truth—and built up a whole consistent geometry on the assumption that *more* than one parallel could be drawn through this point. Then another mathematician constructed a new geometry on the assumption that *no* such parallel could be drawn; and thus there developed flocks of geometries. These have in turn proved useful to physicists. (In quantum theory, I gather, profitable use has been made of an arithmetic in which 2 times 3 does not equal 3 times 2.) Accordingly they too changed their base of operations. Einstein challenged the axiom of simultaneity, that two events can happen in *different* places at the *same* time, and thereby developed his theory of relativity. All along the line physicists have arrived at more satisfactory interpretations of experimental facts by scrapping self-evident truths, breaking the laws of thought —by a systematic exploitation, as it were, of the nonsense that the eighteenth century had triumphantly eliminated. They pride themselves chiefly on the possibility of asking still more preposterous questions and getting still more preposterous answers.

The important contribution of modern physics, then, is not the particular nonsense that it will erect into the truth of tomorrow. It is the junking of Newton's absolutes, the breaking up of his or any other fixed frame of reference, the overthrow of the totalitarian state in the world of thought and the establishment of a democracy in which all hypotheses are freely elected. The revolution might be summarized as the triumph of the postulate over the axiom. An axiom is something self-evident, fixed, unquestioned. A postulate is something assumed, to be tested for its usefulness—not a law laid down by God but a logical fiction consciously invented by man. "No one can say," declared Descartes of the properties of triangles, "that I have invented or imagined them"; mathematicians and scientists now say just this. We must be very careful, writes P. W. Bridgman, that "our present experience does not exact hostages of the future." This might seem too squeamish a concern for posterity, which can be trusted to take care of itself; but scientists are concerned chiefly with their own experience. Newton's assumption of Absolute Time had restricted their outlook and course of action for some two hundred years.

To come to the more specific concepts, it is common news that "matter" is no longer the inert, grossly "material" stuff of old. Physicists now represent objects as processes or events, trace dynamic patterns of an intricacy and subtlety that make the traditional operations of spirit seem crude. The most familiar element in our experience, matter has become more and more elusive, mysterious, incomprehensible. Further, the scientific definition of it is generally conceived as an idealization—a convenient formula, in Bertrand Russell's words, "for describing what happens where it isn't." Strictly, physicists do not know what they are talking about. They do not know what anything *is;* they tell us only what something *does.* Their descriptions are not photographs but ordnance maps for future operations. In a sense, accordingly, they do not so much uncover truth as create it. In *The Evolution of Physics* Einstein talks constantly of the "important invention" of the electromagnetic field and all the other realities "created by modern physics." He rejoices in the new concepts because they have enabled us "to create a more subtle reality"; he would therefore drop them instantly for concepts that made possible a still fancier reality. In other words, the reality known to man is not immutable.

It follows that scientific "laws" are not categorical imperatives. As Karl Pearson pointed out, they are shorthand descriptions of nature and cannot be said to *rule* it. That nature appears to obey them proves nothing, for they were invented for just that purpose; when more experimental returns come in, nature will obey some new, perhaps quite different laws. To give a new twist to the old religious argument, law indeed implies a Lawgiver—who is Man. At any moment, moreover, there are various conceivable ways of interpreting the experimental data. Physicists always prefer the widest possible generalization and the simplest possible formula, seek to break nature down into as few elements and laws as they can; but this procedure is a convenient method, not an absolute necessity. "Nature is pleased with simplicity," Newton wrote, and certainly men are pleased with it; but of nature we cannot be sure. The latest investigations of the subatomic world suggest to physicists as well as laymen that it may be complex beyond the dreams of Marcel Proust.

Implied in these statements is again the human "standpoint." Alfred Korzybski makes out, roughly, three periods in the history of thought: the Greek period, metaphysical and idealistic, in which emphasis was primarily on the observer; the scientific period, semi-empirical and materialistic, in which emphasis was primarily on the thing observed; and the period now dawning, in which knowledge is a transaction between the observer and the observed. On the submicroscopic level, quantum physicists are confirming Coleridge's suspicion of the mechanistic assumption of inert matter that can be observed without being disturbed. The quantum of energy leaving the electron and hitting the observer's eye can be measured only by a new observation, which in turn affects the electron; we cannot actually peep into the private life of the electron. On the cosmic level, Einstein has assumed that absolute time is as meaningless as absolute length or absolute cheese, and that all possible measurements of time and space necessarily involve our position. As Bridgman says, he seized on "the act of the observer as the essence of the situation." The world of Planck and Einstein seems strange, indeed, precisely because man cannot be left out of it. He is not only the most intricate but an indispensable piece of apparatus.

To admit the importance of the observer is also, however, to admit that approximateness is a necessary condition of human knowledge, not merely a matter of imperfect instruments. Uncertainty or mere probability has therefore been erected into a scientific principle. In classical physics one could, in theory, predict with absolute accuracy the future course of any bit of matter if one knew its position and velocity and the forces acting upon it. Heisenberg's Principle of Indeterminacy states that because of the very nature of things we cannot possibly know *both* the position and the velocity of any bit, and that the more precisely we determine the one, the less we must know about the other. Furthermore, in quantum physics there are no laws for the behavior of an individual particle but only statistical averages, "bookkeeping laws," for the behavior of the whole crowd. The physicist cannot even in theory make a definite appointment with a particular electron; he can state merely the probability of where and when it will turn up. He knows that in a certain period approximately so many radium atoms will disintegrate, but he does not know which ones are doomed, or why, or precisely when they will meet their fate. Hence another striking paradox: in this view the lawfulness of nature may be rooted in lawlessness, a very high degree of uniformity resulting only because billions of coins are tossed. What the physicist can state with mathematical exactness is the limits of the *in*exactness of his calculations; as in all operations of pure chance on a large scale, there is a predictable, measurable degree of *in*accuracy.

Now many physicists are dissatisfied with these theories and consider them mere stopgaps. Statistical methods, Bridgman observes, are generally used either to conceal vast ignorance or to simplify vast confusion. Such messy, haphazard behavior of electrons distresses men brought up on law and order; they accordingly look forward to a day when subtler legislation will again induce all the electrons to keep their appointments like little gentlemen. For what is involved here is the fundamental principle of causation. Some physicists regard the surrender of strict causal laws as a threat to the integrity, even the possibility of science. Others agree with Erwin Schroedinger, that cause-and-effect is mere "mechanico-morphism" and should be scrapped with other primitive habits of thought. Still others, such as Einstein and Planck, occupy the middle ground, believing that the traditional formulation of the causal principle is rough and superficial, but that the principle itself is still indispensable to science.

In the face of such distinguished disagreement, it would be brash of a layman to settle the issue. Yet he may wonder whether the concept of cause actually has been given up; the very physicists who argue against it say that we must give it up *because* of such and such facts. What is under fire, at any rate, appears to be only a particular kind of causation, the mechanical concept of classical physics. This was an outgrowth of the common-sense notion of cause as an external force—a notion rooted in our own experience of pushing and pulling, which W. H. George describes as "the triumph of muscle over mind." (Thus the peasant to whom the steam engine was explained asked to see the horse that pulled the locomotive.) The point of the new concepts in physics, however, is that gravitation, for instance, is not a physical something that *makes* apples fall. It is a formula, a concise way of saying that all apples *do* fall, and of linking this fact with other regular sequences. Cause-and-effect may therefore be considered a tautology, a restatement of the observed correlations and uniformities in nature. But however they are described, the important thing is that we can and do make out uniform sequences. The Principle of Indeterminacy applies only to our present *descriptions* of what goes on inside the atom, sets a limit to our possible observation. It does not necessarily apply to the *behavior* of the atom, much less of the stars, or destroy the fundamental assumption of continuity. Whatever they think, in their

actual operations physicists continue to bank on continuity and reg-
ularity.

Hence the layman may safely leave this problem to the experts.
It is significant and healthy that such questions are being raised, in
view of all the "necessities of thought" that have unnecessarily
hampered it, and the answer to questions so stated will not seriously
affect the nature of our knowledge as it is now conceived. Whatever
strict causal laws may be invented will for the physicists still be
working hypotheses, not final truths. "As a matter of fact," wrote
Max Planck, "we have no means whatsoever of proving or disprov-
ing the existence of causation in the external world of nature." And
in any event the causes assigned are always relative and arbitrary,
not absolute and complete, for they never have a beginning or end.
The scientist stops at some point, behind which one can always go
in search of still larger or deeper causes—the cause, say, of gravitation. Thus John Smith explains a noise by saying that little Willie
just smashed a plate, and he disposes of the problem by spanking
Willie. He could also make this cause the beginning of an endless
analysis, leading through the laws of sound and the psychology of
Willie to the whole content of human knowledge, the whole history
of the human race. Any single event involves the entire system in
which it takes place. Finally one is asking, what is the "cause" of
the universe?

Strictly, such questions are meaningless; and they have tormented
men for ages. If nature abhors a vacuum, then men are indeed
children of nature. They must somehow fill in all the empty spaces
in their picture of the world—just as the anguished Victorians could
not bear the sight of a blank wall and cluttered up their rooms with
bric-a-brac. The idea of an infinite, eternal universe has always
troubled them, for they must have a beginning and an end; the idea
of a finite universe has troubled them no less, for it leaves the im-
ponderable emptiness beyond the borders of space and before the
beginning of time. They then try to explain the inexplicable by giving it a capitalized name—the First Cause, the Prime Mover, Fate,
God. Somehow they must provide a mechanism, find a reason why,
justify or dignify what simply *is*. And modern science is distinguished by the calm acceptance of empty spaces, the calm aware-

ness of the meaningless question—with the realization that to call a question meaningless is to make a significant statement about nature and the operations of the human mind. "What?" and "Why?" may stimulate scientific research, but they do not, strictly constitute its subject matter. Its spirit is a thorough-going pragmatism.

This attitude results in part from the assumption that process and energy, not matter, is the fundamental fact; if one thinks of existence as activity rather than being, he is less likely to ask how the universe "came into being." But it results as well from the realization that pure reason cannot take us to the heart of reality. If all flubjubs are dingbats and this is a flubjub, then it must also be a dingbat. This syllogism, Ogden and Richards point out, carries absolute conviction; but it proves nothing about the existence of dingbats. Formal logic can never prove the truth of its premises. Man can never be certain that his logic is the logic of things, that the scheme of science represents nature completely and represents nothing else. For all human purposes man is in fact the measure of the universe; but nobody knows exactly what it is he is measuring. In the past, scientists forced on nature the limitations of the human mind, identifying their picture of reality with reality itself. Now physicists recognize that this was but a subtler form of the ancient anthropomorphic habit; man was simply creating nature in his own image. So, indeed, he must if he is to deal with it at all. But for efficient dealings he must also be aware of what he is doing.

This article makes a key distinction between attitudes of modern and traditional scientists by using the phrase "human standpoint." You are, of course, no modern scientist; yet you have recently concluded an activity—measuring the wind—that was at least faintly scientific, and you are after all as modern a person as any scientist. What about *your* "human standpoint"? As you think over your experience with your anemometer in Theme 12, can you see yourself as limited by a human standpoint that is finally "anthropomorphic" in Muller's sense?

To answer this question, you might begin by addressing yourself to several other questions that can be made up from the phraseology of Muller's article. "Strictly," he says (page 133), "physicists do not know what they are talking about." Is there a way in which you can see yourself as not knowing what you were talking about in Theme 12—an ignorance that had nothing to do with the crudity of your instrument or your innocence about meteorology? What does "strictly" mean here? Again (same paragraph): "They do not so much uncover truth as create it." Were you in any way a creator of truth? Muller's emphasis is on "the act of the observer as the essence of the situation." Can your situation be seen in that way, so that your act of observing becomes its "essence"? Implied in such a discussion is a special meaning of "truth"—that is, as something not "uncovered" but "created." Can an appropriate definition of *wind* be proposed in similar terms, and on the basis of your own experience with wind in Theme 12?

DIRECTIONS FOR THEME 13

RESEE YOUR EXPERIENCE WITH YOUR ANEMOMETER (THEME 12) BY RECONSIDERING AND ANALYZING IT IN THE LIGHT OF THE "HUMAN STANDPOINT" OF MULLER'S ARTICLE. CONCLUDE YOUR ANALYSIS WITH A CAREFUL DEFINITION OF "WIND"—A DEFINITION THAT IS DIRECTLY RELATED TO THE THEME YOU HAVE JUST COMPOSED.

14

A LETTER TO A CONGRESSMAN

There's no place I can go in the Pentagon to get objective information.

—CONGRESSMAN MAHON (TEXAS)

The reading of anemometers—the reading of anything—can be a matter of life and death. On April 23, 1958, at an army camp in Kentucky, five parachutists were killed and at least 137 injured during a mass drop by the 101st Airborne Division. Wind did it. The next day the following front-page lead article about the disaster appeared in a New York City newspaper. Read it critically, trying to understand it in the light of what you have learned about wind and anemometers, and the "human standpoint."

Army Debated Winds Before Jump—
Congressional Inquiry Is Pushed

Special to the New York Post

Fort Campbell, Ky., April 24—Was it too dangerous to jump? The question was debated at 4 a.m. yesterday, hours before units

From the *New York Post,* April 24, 1958. Reprinted by permission of New York Post. Copyright 1958 by New York Post Corporation.

of the famed 101st Airborne Division were ordered to leap, and it still was debated today after five were dead and 137 injured in the mass jump.

The danger point for the wind is 12 knots per hour. The Fort Campbell public information officer on the ground told reporters the wind had reached that point just before the mass leap.

But today Maj. Gen. W. C. Westmoreland, commander of the famed 101st and himself one of the 'chutists, insisted the wind never went beyond 10 knots.

The actual jump was made at 10 a.m., six hours after the decision had been reached.

A board of inquiry was to investigate the question. Pentagon sources told The Post today, however, that the investigation would be strictly local and that no Washington inquiry was planned.

However, pressure was coming from Congress for a more extensive investigation. Rep. Walter Norblad (R-Ore.) called for the House Armed Services Committee—of which he is a member—to look into the jump.

Rep. Santangelo (D-N.Y.) agreed. He said:

"In times of peace an accident like this seems incredible. I suppose there is some human error involved. I think the committee should find out who is responsible."

But the committee's chairman of investigations, Rep. Hebert (D-La.), said he would "not permit any such investigation.

"I don't know all the facts, but what is there to investigate?" he told The Post.

"It was just an accident. The Army certainly isn't killing off its own boys and I can see no point to it."

The weather was gusty through the night preceding the jump, and Westmoreland called a meeting at 4 a.m. yesterday with Col. Charles W. Howe, commander of the airplanes scheduled to carry the 'chutists.

"We had to make a decision then whether to jump or not," Westmoreland said.

The weather forecast was for wind only up to 10 knots, and so the order went out:

Jump.

The men jumped. As they scattered across the countryside outside the jump area, the cries of "medic, medic" piped across the fields and rocks. And then the mistake was realized.

Today, the Army announced it would stage an even bigger jump in the same area Saturday, using the same 101st Airborne (which supplied the troops for Little Rock's integration enforcement), but not the same men.

The actual toll of yesterday's leap included almost all of the 1,400 men involved. The 137 most seriously injured were hospitalized; the others were released after first-aid treatment for bruises and scratches.

As they descended on the drop zone, two miles long and 1¼ miles wide, the wind gusts filled their parachutes and dragged them across ground studded with tree stumps, rock outcroppings, mud puddles and graveled areas.

The dead were believed to have been dashed head-first against rocks and trees. Several might have been strangled by the suspension cords of their billowing 'chutes.

The facts underlying the disaster were expected to be disclosed with the start today of a routine investigation by the commander of Fort Campbell. Such an investigation is customary, according to the Pentagon.

"Our safety factors are arrived at through considerable experience," an Army spokesman said. "We've been jumping on the drop zone for a long time."

The Army cited its safety record for paratroop practice jumps. It said that in 1954 there were three deaths and 539 injuries in 183,900 recorded jumps; in 1955 there were four deaths and 772 injuries in 357,800 jumps; in 1956 there were four deaths and 474 injuries in 222,900 jumps and last year there were four deaths and 434 injuries in 238,100 jumps.

Even before the first of the paratroopers began bailing out of the giant Air Force transports overhead, Army officers standing in the drop zone said the wind was blowing at 12 knots per hour—the official danger point, according to reporters who accompanied them.

"The injuries sustained resulted from an increased wind velocity or gusts following the drop," Westmoreland said.

The general's statement was issued by Maj. Lou Breault, chief public information officer at Fort Campbell, who was one of those standing in the drop zone.

Breault said the wind velocity readings were taken by an ane-mometer (wind velocity indicator) on the large "T" laid out on the drop zone to mark the release point for paratroopers in the air above.

Reporters, however, said Breault was one of the officers who told them that the wind velocity already had reached 12 knots when the planes bearing the paratroopers came overhead.

"They said the wind was blowing harder when they jumped than they were told it would be," reported Carl May of the Nashville Tennesseean.

"They were told that the wind would be from 6 to 10 knots. But Breault himself told me at least once out there on the field that it was 12."

Even before he learned that there had been any fatalities, West-moreland, battling the wind in his 70th parachute jump, said after his descent that he would cancel any additional drops if they were scheduled for yesterday.

The 44-year-old major general, the youngest of his rank in the Army, conceded that the wind was stronger than he had anticipated. Then he indicated that there had been some apprehension about the wind at least six hours before the mass jump.

Westmoreland disclosed that at 4 a.m. yesterday he called a meet-ing with Col. Charles W. Howe, commander of the Air Force group which was to ferry the men from Seward Air Force base in Smyrna, Tenn.

"We had to make a decision as to whether to jump or not," ex-plained the general, who added that the meeting was called after receipt of weather reports showing that the wind velocity would approach gusts of 10 knots.

"The decision was made. It was to jump."

It was some time after Westmoreland made these statements that he learned of the deaths and the injuries.

The general, who took command of the 101st only a few weeks ago, himself was dragged along several hundred yards over a gravel road before he could collapse his 'chute. But he escaped uninjured.

"I just couldn't run as fast as my 'chute was going," he said.

Although many remained tightlipped and grim-faced and tried to limp stoically to their assembly areas, other 'chutists described the exercise, called Operation Eagle Wing, with some bitterness.

"Everything hit me," said Pvt. John Mass. "I had a long ride on a short drop zone. I wished I had landed in a tree. It would have been softer."

"It was windy when we jumped but it was worse on the ground," said Pvt. John Castro of Silver Springs, Md., who came down against a log pile.

"I just got bumped around.

"The guy next to me was killed.

"Everyone was telling me I was very lucky. It could have been me."

Yesterday's jump was the first of its kind, according to the Army. All the heavy equipment needed to fight a battle in an atomic war was sent down by parachute with the 1,400 men, and the emphasis was on speed.

It took only 20 minutes to unload the air transports and cargo ships.

Although Army officers standing on the drop zone could see 'chutists running into trouble as they hit ground, no one realized that the difficulty was so widespread or drastic.

"You can't see from one end of the drop zone to the other," explained Maj. Breault, who himself helped two paratroopers collapse their 'chutes.

"The fact that you see one or two men hurt doesn't mean it's happening all over. There is no method of predicting gusts at ground level. It can be gusty in one part of a drop zone and not in another."

At the U. S. Weather Bureau in Washington, forecasters agreed that very often an anemometer might record one wind velocity in one part of an airfield while wind gusts jump to greater strengths in other parts of the same field.

"There might be a reading of six knots at one end of the runway," one meteorologist said, "and an airliner might encounter 15 knots at the other end—or worse!"

Breault said in addition that if conditions in the drop zone become hazardous, a red smoke grenade is released by a safety officer on the ground. This warns paratroopers above not to jump.

In yesterday's mass drop, however, Breault insisted that there was not sufficient reason for the safety officer to set off the red grenade.

Reports of the deaths and widespread injuries did not come in until after the jump had been completed, he said.

But May, the reporter from the Nashville Tennesseean, said that as soon as the men began to hit the ground, it was obvious that the wind was carrying many of them out of the drop zone.

With the emphasis on speed, however, he said there wouldn't have been time to stop the remainder of the paratroopers from jumping.

News of the deaths and injuries brought a flood of phone calls from relatives of men stationed at the fort. Telephone company switchboards in Hopkinsville and Clarksville, two nearby cities, reported no circuits available for two hours last night.

The most seriously injured—many with broken limbs—were taken to the base hospital at the fort. Others were treated at an emergency hospital set up on the drop zone.

There are a number of questions you should want to ask in your effort to understand this article; some of them are probably unanswerable. But let us begin with an obvious one. When the officers standing in the drop zone "said the wind was blowing at 12 knots per hour," just what do you suppose their statement meant? How would you want to qualify it; what further questions would you want to ask them? (Who did exactly what, exactly when and where, before *seeing* wind as "12 knots"?) The article seems to imply that only one anemometer was used; does it suggest where that anemometer was located? Your experience with your own instrument and your reading of Shaw (Theme 12) should encourage further questioning. For example, what evidence can you find in the article about the total size of the drop zone, and what further skepticism does its size suggest as to the meaning or reliability of the phrase "wind velocity" in the context of the article?

In writing Theme 14 you are to focus on the remark of Rep. Santangelo (D-N.Y.): "In times of peace an accident like this seems incredible. I suppose there is some human error involved. I think the committee should find out who is responsible." Your general problem is to say something to Mr. Santangelo, on the basis of what you have recently learned in Themes 12 and 13, that might be of use to him in carrying out his responsibilities as a congressman. Could you, for example, give him some suggestions for finding out "who is responsible"? How could he go about finding out? On the basis of the evidence you have, was "human error" involved, and if so, whose? What suggestions could you give him for improving the safety of mass drops? Finally, what about his remark that "an accident like this seems incredible"? Explain to him why, in the light of what you have learned about wind and the human standpoint, it is *not* incredible, but all too credible. Tell him something, in other words, about the nature of seeing.

DIRECTIONS FOR THEME 14

WRITE A LETTER TO CONGRESSMAN SANTANGELO IN WHICH YOU EXPLAIN TO HIM SOME OF THE COMPLICATIONS IN THE REPORT OF THE DISASTER AT FORT CAMPBELL, AND SUGGEST TO HIM SOME PROCEDURES FOR UNDERSTANDING AND PERHAPS EVEN AVOIDING SUCH INCIDENTS IN THE FUTURE.

15   THE WRITER'S ART

How much we are the woods we wander in.
—RICHARD WILBUR

The article that follows is by a distinguished physicist at Harvard who has already been referred to more than once in this book—P. W. Bridgman. Some of the statements made by Muller in Theme 13 about the revolution in physics you will now find corroborated by a genuine physicist talking about his trade. This article is a summary of an address Mr. Bridgman gave early in 1950 to an academic society in Boston. It is not easy reading, but if you find yourself in difficulties it may be sobering to remember that an educated audience was expected to follow it as delivered orally to them a single time.

Your problem in this final assignment is to relate some of Bridgman's terms in this address to problems you have experienced in this course of exercises, or in other words to find a parallel between the modern physicist's situation and your own as a writer, a composer of themes.

Philosophical Implications of Physics

by P. W. BRIDGMAN

It is common knowledge that since the turn of the century the physicist has passed through what amounts to an intellectual crisis forced by the discovery of experimental facts of a sort which he had not previously envisaged, and which he would not even have thought possible. These new facts were in the first instance in the realm of relativity phenomena, and only later in the quantum realm. It was the relativity phenomena, that is, the phenomena in the realms of high velocities, that had the chief influence in modifying the conceptual outlook of the physicist. Some of these effects were highly paradoxical, and included such effects as meter sticks whose length changed when they were set in motion, clocks which ran slow when moving, and weights which became heavier when moving. In fact, these effects were so paradoxical and contrary to common sense that some physicists and most men in the street refused to accept them and even sought to throw them out of court by ridicule. But the facts refused to be thrown out of court, and the paradoxes were presently resolved by Einstein's theory of relativity. This theory embraced in the first place the mathematical theory by which all the facts were correlated into a single mathematical structure. But no less notable as an intellectual achievement and equally essential to the removal of paradox was Einstein's handling of the physical concepts which entered the mathematical edifice. It in this latter which is our concern this evening. There were two aspects to Einstein's handling of the physical concepts. There was in the first place a realization that the paradoxes involved primarily questions of meaning and that the common sense meanings of the physical terms such as length and time were not sharp enough to serve in the new physical situations. In the second place there was

From the American Academy of Arts and Sciences *Bulletin*, III, 5 (February, 1950). Reprinted by permission of the Academy and the author.

the method by which the necessary increased sharpness was im-
parted to meanings. This method was to specify the operations
which were involved in concrete instances in applying the term
whose meaning is in question.

The attitude toward meanings which eliminated the paradoxes
of relativity theory has been carried over by the physicist into all
the rest of physics, particularly into the new realm of quantum
phenomena, where it is absolutely essential to any valid thinking at
all. The physicist has come to see that the common sense meanings
of many of his terms as he has adapted them from the daily life of
common sense are not precise nor unique, but are really multiple
and apply to a number of different procedures. . . .

The technique by which the physicist makes himself conscious of
the multiple meanings of many of his terms is a technique which
can be carried over with profit into the situations of daily life. This
technique we have seen consists of an analysis of the operations
which are used in applying the term in concrete instances. If it
should turn out that different operations are used in different circumstances to define what is ostensibly the same term, then precision in the use of language demands that we should recognize the
difference by inventing new terms to cover the recognizably different operations. It will turn out on examination that nearly all our
abstract terms have multiple meanings. For instance, "democracy"
as used by a Russian does not have the same meaning as when used
by an American. The reason that it does not have the same meaning is that what the Russian does to determine whether a given
society is democratic is not the same as what the American does.
The Russian asks whether on election day any citizen may go to the
polls and mark a cross opposite the only name on the ballot, a name
which was placed there by the single party which directs the affairs
of the country. The American on the other hand asks whether on
election day the citizen may go to the polls and mark a cross opposite
his choice of several names on the ballot, which were placed there
by one or the other of several parties, in one of which he himself
may have played a role in selecting the name. Since the operations
for determining whether a given society is a democracy or not are
different, the meaning of the term itself is different, and properly

two different words should be used. The retention of a single term
leads only to confusion, a confusion which may be willfully culti-
vated by those who can profit by it.

A consciousness of the presumptive inadequacy of the common
terms which are the unthinking intellectual legacy of the race should
be continually with us, and should impart a definite bias to all the
thinking of a modern man. In fact, it seems to me that no one
should feel himself educated until he has acquired this bias, and
one of the primary objects of a truly liberal education should be to
impart it.

Suppose now that my proselytizing has been effective enough to
make a man embark on an operational analysis of his meanings, what
is involved? He will obviously need to be able to specify what the
operations are that he uses to give his meanings. He will find almost
at once that there are different sorts of operation—operations on
different levels. Let us consider first the operations of the physicist.
To be specific, what are the operations by which he gives meaning
to "length"? We need not go into full detail here, but it is obvious
that his is an operation of measurement, and as such it is performed
with a certain instrument, in this case a meter stick. We may, then,
recognize in general a level of instrumental operations or laboratory
operations. But it is obvious that the operation of measuring a length
is not exclusively an operation with the meter stick, because we have
to count the number of times the meter stick is applied, and the
operation of counting is one that we do in our heads and not with
an instrument, although perhaps we could. We recognize, therefore,
another great class of operations beside the instrumental, namely
mental operations. I believe that examination would disclose that
the meanings of the larger part of the terms which the physicist
uses are to be found in mental operations. This I believe to be true
in even greater degree of the terms of daily life. Comparatively few
of these terms find their meanings through simple direct "objective"
operations in the "external" world in the way that the instrumental
operations of the physicist find their meaning. Of the terms that
do thus find their meaning the best examples are the names of
things, such as "cat" or "tree." But abstract nouns find their mean-

ings through operations which are almost exclusively mental. These mental operations, furthermore, are in large degree of a special type which are not especially important for the physicist, namely verbal operations. Verbal operations are a particular sort of verbal behavior. Verbal behavior is such a universal characteristic of man that it must be recognized that he has a verbal as well as a physical environment. In this verbal environment complex patterns of behavior occur, which for any individual in a given culture may have all the appearance of compulsion and inevitability that the patterns forced on him by his external objective environment do. Corresponding to this verbal compulsion and inevitability, verbal operations are possible which may be performed with as little uncertainty as the operations of the physical world.

What now is the significance of a term whose meaning has thus been fixed in terms of verbal operations? I think it is obvious that it may have varying kinds and degrees of significance. In the first place, man's verbal environment is a product of evolution continually subject to the restriction that it have survival value, so that the presumption is that there is a fairly good correspondence between the verbal world and the physical world. It follows that one may make experiments in the verbal environment and then transfer the results of these experiments to the physical environment with rather good prospects of success. It is, I think, a rather common human trait to deal with the physical environment in such a verbal fashion; it is more likely to be the method the more novel or unfamiliar the physical situation. Observation inclines me to the belief that it is the method by which many women deal with mechanical situations. But I believe that it will be conceded that it is less satisfactory than more direct methods.

It is, I think, the tacit implication in most language that eventually meanings can be made to emerge from the verbal environment and make connection with something more concrete and physical, and our verbal usages are based on this presupposition. In many cases, however, explicit analysis has not been made to find whether such nonverbal emergence can in fact be made to occur. When the analysis is made, I believe it will often be found, particularly with regard to abstract terms, that such emergence does not occur. It is not surprising that this should be the case, because the evolution of our abstract terms has been subject to no such drastic survival criterion as have our commoner terms, but they have often been subject only to the requirement that they produce in our fellows the reaction that we want. Since this reaction is in many cases merely some specific social behavior, words get fastened in language without necessarily having any objective physical reference. This is particularly the case if the social behavior which it was intended to evoke by the use of the word is itself merely verbal behavior. This is the case in many, perhaps most, of our social situations. Everyone is predisposed to it by the character of our elementary education, for usually the only check which is applied to a child to find whether he has grasped an idea or caught a meaning is to see whether he makes the proper verbal reaction.

It seems to me that a man is not properly educated to grapple with the problems of our age unless he understands at least two things about his verbal environment. The first is the extreme complexity of the verbal structure which man has erected. Man has always been the builder: of verbal structures no less than of pyramids and great walls of China. Within this verbal environment it is possible for people to live together with agreement, each member of society acting according to patterns of behavior which his neighbor can predict. Often the ability to be able to predict verbal behavior is the only criterion imposed for a satisfactory verbalism, and the fact that it satisfies this criterion is no guarantee that it will have validity in the external physical world, although many verbalisms do have such physical validity. The second thing which I believe that a modern man must have to be educated to cope with his verbal environment is a knowledge of the results of an operational analysis of the important abstract terms used by the culture in which he lives. It is particularly important that he know what terms are capable of eventual emergence into the "objective," or physical, and those which are not capable of such eventual emergence but find their meaning only in terms of a regress which never leaves the verbal level. In other words, it is important that he know where are the open verbal chains. I believe that it will be found that these open verbal chains are much commoner than a complacent humanity likes to believe.

The operational attitude toward meanings is only one aspect of the operational point of view in general. This is to see the world in terms of activities rather than in terms of things. If one adopts this point of view, then much of what we have been saying about meanings becomes tautological, for meanings under this point of view would automatically be expressed in terms of some sort of activity, that is, some sort of operation. The significance of the operational attitude toward meanings then is to be found in the analysis into specific operations in concrete cases, for our experience then enables us to judge whether the specific operations are of value for the purposes we have in mind.

Common sense analyzes the world into objects which in greater or less degree are endowed with stability and permanence. Common sense accepts this analysis for its purposes as an ultimate analysis, and treats its objects as the ultimate components of "reality." Now this is no reproach to common sense, because every analysis has to stop somewhere, because of the finite duration of human life if for no other reason. The only question we have to ask with regard to any specific restricted analysis is whether it goes far enough to meet the demands that we shall put upon it.

It is true that for most of the purposes of daily life we do not need to analyze beyond the concept of object, but this is by no means the situation in the new realm of quantum phenomena which experiment has opened to the physicist. Here the common-sense notions of object completely fail us; there is no permanence or stability, experiments cannot be exactly repeated, measurements cannot be made in the conventional way, the very attribute of identity, which is perhaps the ultimate criterion of an object, becomes meaningless. Although we cannot deal with such situations by the methods of common sense, we are perforce constrained to deal with them as best we can and not ignore them defeatistly. What is more, the theoretical physicist has worked out a way of handling these situations which is highly satisfactory, as shown by the range of new phenomena which he has got under control. This method involves an analysis into activities, and most of these activities are in the paper-and-pencil domain and involve the manipulations of mathematical symbols according to rules many of which were evolved to meet the occasion.

Taken altogether, it seems to me that it is a simple matter of observation that an analysis of the world about us into activities goes beyond an analysis into objects. Furthermore, at the present epoch, an analysis into activities is adequate for the purposes of the physicist and as far as I can judge for the purposes of other natural scientists as well. Whether the poet and the artist would accept it as adequate in their domain I cannot pretend to say; but this is perhaps of little moment, because the poet and the artist, insofar as they are concerned with creating and not with philosophizing about what they are creating, have little traffic with analysis. The point of view which sees the world in terms of activity is closely related to the philosophical point of view set forth in the recent book by Dewey and Bentley entitled, "Knowing and the Known.". . .

It seems to me that our attitude toward many social institutions will be essentially modified if we see the world as activity. Consider for example the state and our attitude toward it. Viewed as activity, it will be impossible to think of the state as some super thing or even super person with an existence of its own. For analysis of what happens whenever we are concerned with any functioning of the state discloses that we are always concerned with the activities of individuals. Every law of the state has originated in one way or another in the actions of individuals—in a democracy by the majority vote of the individual members of a legislature, or in a dictatorship by the decree of the individual who is dictator. If I violate the law, I may be arrested by the order of some individual police captain to this or that policeman to go to my house and compel me by the display of superior force to come with him. And if I am tried and condemned, it is by some individual judge who decides by his own individual judgment what interpretation should be put upon the laws inscribed on the statute books when applied to my particular case. There is no mechanism by which the state functions except through the activities of individuals.

It may seem to many that such a realistic attitude can lead only to anarchy and chaos, and it must be admitted that there is such danger in the process of transition. But it seems to me that on the other hand it is only by adopting such a realistic view that we can hope for the development of that new ethics for which the present need is so crying and obvious, a need so new that none of the great traditional systems of ethics have adequately anticipated it.

Finally, I come to what it seems to me may well be from the long-range point of view the most revolutionary of the insights to be derived from our recent experiences in physics, more revolutionary than the insights afforded by the discoveries of Galileo and Newton or of Darwin. This is the insight that it is impossible to transcend the human reference point. The history of much of philosophy and most of religion has been the history of the attempt of the human race to transcend its own reference point by the invention of essences and absolutes and realities and existences. It should have been obvious enough, even without the experience of recent physics, that this was an impossible attempt. For even the mystic, convinced of direct communication between his soul and some supernatural external reality, would have had to admit that it was his soul, and therefore a human soul, that had the experience, and that the experience took place in his consciousness, and therefore a human consciousness. But considerations like these are so obvious that it is easy to overlook their significance. Recent experience in physics documents in another way the conclusion that it is impossible to transcend the human reference point, and by the emphasis of novelty may perhaps succeed in injecting this insight into the backbone of humanity. The new insight comes from a realization that the structure of nature may eventually be such that our processes of thought do not correspond to it sufficiently to permit us to think about it at all. We have already had an intimation of this in the behavior of very small things in the quantum domain. We have seen that in this domain there are no longer things, in the sense that a thing has individuality and identity and recurs in experience. I can conceive of no more fundamental need of thought than the need for identity and recurrence. Memory would be impossible without the background that identifies what is occurring in our minds now with something that has happened before. No operational analysis would

be possible if we could not identify our operations. Without identification our mental activities would be as amorphous as we imagine
must be the first experiences of a baby just born, or perhaps rather
considerably unborn. The structure of nature in the direction of the
very small is simply not the same as the structure of our thought;
and, being so, it is meaningless even to attempt to formulate what
it is like.

Similarly we meet a possible incompatibility between the structure of nature and our thought in the direction of the very large.
This emergency is not yet actually upon us, but the possibility can
be seen around the next corner. If the giant telescope at Palomar
should indicate that the universe does not fade out but is open in
the direction of the very large, we are going to be seriously em-
barrassed to find the proper way of thinking about it. The reason is
that it is fundamental to all our theoretical thinking in physics to
be able to divide the universe into two parts, one the part under
investigation, and the other the rest of the universe, which is the
seat of the observer but otherwise neutral. If the universe is actually
open, it will not be legitimate to think of the rest of the universe as
neutral, and we will lose the basis for the most sweeping generaliza-
tions that we have—the conservation of energy and the inexorable
increase of entropy.

There may be differences of opinion about the seriousness of the
intellectual dilemma that may be waiting for us in the direction of
the very large, but there can be no difference of opinion with regard
to the dilemma that now confronts us in the direction of the very small.
We are now approaching a bound beyond which we are forever
estopped from pushing our inquiries, not by the construction of the
world, but by the construction of ourselves. The world fades out and
eludes us because it becomes meaningless. We cannot even express
this in the way we would like. We cannot say that there exists a
world beyond any knowledge possible to us because of the nature of
knowledge. The very concept of existence becomes meaningless. It
is literally true that the only way of reacting to this is to shut up. We
are confronted with something truly ineffable. We have reached the
limit of the vision of the great pioneers of science, the vision, namely,
that we live in a sympathetic world, in that it is comprehensible by

our minds. It seems to me that the impact of a realization of this will be more momentous than was ever the impact of the vision of Newton or Darwin.

Your object in Theme 15 is to try applying some of these statements about problems in modern physics to your own problems as a writer. To do this we will concentrate on a few sentences from Bridgman's address:

Finally, I come to what seems to me may well be from the long range point of view the most revolutionary of the insights to be derived from our recent experiments in physics, more revolutionary than the insights afforded by the discoveries of Galileo and Newton, or Darwin. This is the insight that it is impossible to transcend the human reference point. . . . The new insight comes from a realization that the structure of nature may eventually be such that our processes of thought do not correspond to it sufficiently to permit us to think about it at all. . . . We are now approaching a bound beyond which we are forever estopped from pushing our inquiries, not by the construction of the world, but by the construction of ourselves. The world fades out and eludes us because it becomes meaningless. We cannot even express this in the way we would like. We cannot say that there exists a world beyond any knowledge possible to us because of the nature of knowledge. It is literally true that the only way of reacting to this is to shut up. We are confronted with something truly ineffable. We have reached the limit of vision of the great pioneers of science, the vision, namely, that we live in a sympathetic world in that it is comprehensible by our minds.

Your final theme assignment now asks you to relate some of Bridgman's terms to your own efforts at seeing and saying. You may not be a physicist at the frontiers of science, but you are (or should be) at the frontiers of your own means of expression. You too have a "human reference point" you cannot transcend; this assignment asks you to determine where that point is.

DIRECTIONS FOR THEME 15

SELECT AND DESCRIBE A PARTICULAR EXPERIENCE OF YOURS AS
A WRITER OF THESE THEMES, IN WHICH YOU FELT STOPPED
(OR "ESTOPPED") FROM PUSHING YOUR INQUIRIES FURTHER.
EXPLAIN WHAT YOU WERE TRYING TO DO, AND TRY TO POINT OUT
JUST WHERE, HOW, AND WHY YOU WERE STOPPED. MAKE WHAT
USE YOU CAN OF BRIDGMAN'S TERMS, SUCH AS "THE HUMAN
REFERENCE POINT," "THE CONSTRUCTION OF THE WORLD," AND
"THE CONSTRUCTION OF OURSELVES." WHAT MEANS IF ANY DO
YOU HAVE AT YOUR DISPOSAL, AS A WRITER, TO CONFRONT A
WORLD THAT IS NOT SYMPATHETIC IN THAT IT IS NOT COMPRE-
HENSIBLE TO YOUR MIND? DO YOU SHUT UP? WHY OR WHY NOT?
CONCLUDE WITH A FINAL STATEMENT ON THE NATURE OF THE
WRITER'S ART AS YOU HAVE EXPERIENCED IT IN THESE EXER-
CISES.

Perhaps you can see from the poem by Robert Frost on the opposite page that your "final statement" need not be a negative
one.

For Once, Then, Something

by ROBERT FROST

Others taunt me with having knelt at well-curbs
Always wrong to the light, so never seeing
Deeper down in the well than where the water
Gives me back in a shining surface picture
Me myself in the summer heaven godlike
Looking out of a wreath of fern and cloud-puffs.
Once, when trying with chin against a well-curb,
I discerned, as I thought, beyond the picture,
Through the picture, a something white, uncertain,
Something more of the depths—and then I lost it.
Water came to rebuke the too clear water.
One drop fell from a fern, and lo, a ripple
Shook whatever it was lay there at bottom,
Blurred it, blotted it out. What was that whiteness?
Truth? A pebble of quartz? For once, then, something.